Accounting and Financial Globalization

Accounting and Financial Globalization

Joshua Ronen,
Editor-in-Chief

Joshua Livnat,
Associate Editor

PUBLISHED UNDER THE AUSPICES OF
THE JOURNAL OF ACCOUNTING, AUDITING, & FINANCE

Sponsored by the Vincent C. Ross Institute of Accounting Research,
Stern School of Business, New York University,

The New York University School of Law, and

Touche Ross and Co. (now Deloitte & Touche)

Q

QUORUM BOOKS

New York • Westport, Connecticut • London

Library of Congress Cataloging-in-Publication Data

Accounting and financial globalization / Joshua Ronen, editor in chief ;
  Joshua Livnat, associate editor ; sponsored by the Vincent C.
  Ross Institute of Accounting Research . . . [et al.].
      p.   cm.
      "Published under the auspices of the Journal of accounting,
  auditing, and finance."
      Includes bibliographical references and index.
      ISBN 0-89930-618-7 (alk. paper)
      1. International business enterprises—Accounting.   2. Capital
  movements—Mathematical models.   3. Interest rates—Mathematical
  models.   4. Uncertainty—Mathematical models.   5. Transborder data
  flow.   I. Ronen, Joshua.   II. Livnat, Joshua.   III. Vincent C. Ross
  Institute of Accounting Research.   IV. Journal of accounting, auditing, and
  finance.   V. Title: Financial globalization.
  HF5686.I56A24   1991
  657'.48—dc20   90-26406

British Library Cataloguing in Publication Data is available.

Library of Congress Catalog Card Number: 90-26406
ISBN: 0-89930-618-7

First published in 1991

Quorum Books, 88 Post Road West, Westport, CT 06881
An imprint of Greenwood Publishing Group, Inc.

Printed in the United States of America

The paper used in this book complies with the
Permanent Paper Standard issued by the National
Information Standards Organization (Z39.48-1984).

10 9 8 7 6 5 4 3 2 1

Contents

Introduction

GLOBALIZATION OF CAPITAL MARKETS

The twentieth century has been characterized by two dramatic improvements in the environment that have had direct implications for business practices: (1) The beginning of the century was characterized by major advances in transportation and infrastructure, and (2) the past two decades of this century were characterized by great improvements in communications within and across countries. Both areas of improvement radically changed business practices in the direction of internationalization of business operations.

With the improvements in transportation, businesses found that they could penetrate areas that were previously unprofitable due to high transportation costs. For example, with the widespread use of automobiles and roads, areas that previously could have been reached only by boats or by other slow means of transportation became accessible for marketing as well as manufacturing. With the development of air transportation, business people found traveling long distances substantially more rapid and the possibility of fast supply of merchandise using air freight much more affordable.

With advances in technology, including space technology and satellites, communication between and within countries became faster and much cheaper. It is very difficult to imagine business operations today without sophisticated telephone networking facilities, fax machines, and electronic mail. Clearly, it is hardly relevant today where an executive's office is located if the executive has access to means of communication with others within (or outside) the business organization.

These major improvements in transportation and communication contributed directly to the globalization of business operations. This globalization took various forms. On the most basic level, businesses found it easier and more convenient to market products beyond their home country. Firms could produce their products in one country (where input factors were cheaper) and market the products in the home and foreign countries. Different steps in the manufacturing process could be done in different countries. Finally, firms could form business relationships that cut across country lines; two or more firms from different countries could cooperate in a joint venture in still another country in an attempt to maximize efficiency of operations.

With the ever-increasing internationalization of businesses, problems of financing became more and more difficult; creditors and investors were required to examine business deals that spanned beyond the local environment. Assessments of foreign economic environments became more and more crucial, as did understanding of business practices in other countries. Firms are now turning more and more to investors and creditors in one country in an attempt to secure financing for operations in another country. These investors and creditors may require different information about these firms than would be required about firms that operate in the local environment alone.

The main question addressed by the following studies is how information could aid investors in international or foreign firms. The five studies examine different aspects of this question using different research methodologies and approaches. Miller and Copeland examine whether the disclosure of additional information is socially desirable. Branson and Jaffee examine the effects of various degrees of information about local and foreign investments on the demand and risk of securities. Adler and Prasad look at the optimal foreign currency hedging of investors in international portfolios and the effects of information on the demand for hedging. Geman, Savanayana, and Schneeweis present an empirical study of the effects of foreign information on the variability of prices in the local market as compared to the effects of local information. Finally, Darrough and Harris examine the effects of a particular form of a business practice in one country (management forecasts in Japan) on local markets and compare their results with those obtained in another setting (voluntary forecasts in the United States).

One of the major questions faced by international regulatory bodies is the issue of whether to harmonize information disclosures about corporations operating in different countries. Harmonization here refers to the imposition of uniform accounting standards to be applied and of disclosures within and without the formal set of financial statements.

Generally, required information disclosure sets imposed in Asia and Europe seem to be a subset of the disclosure sets required or voluntarily made available in the United States. At least with respect to Asia, the study by Choi and Ronen (1988)[1] concluded that financial disclosure in

1. Frederick D. S. Choi and Joshua Ronen, "Financial Disclosure Policy in a Global Capital

Asia has not yet obtained levels found in the United States. Hence, the harmonization of accounting information or other disclosures amounts within most countries other than the United States to increasing public disclosure. As a result, the evaluation of harmonization boils down to the examination of the effect of enhanced public disclosure on the welfare of participants in the marketplace.

This is the primary question addressed by Miller and Copeland in this volume. Under Miller and Copeland's model, disclosure of additional public information leads to a higher fraction of informed traders and it improves welfare. As in other models of this type, Miller and Copeland's analysis features both liquidity traders and nonliquidity traders holding portfolios of risky stock and a riskless fund. The behavior of liquidity traders is exogenous, but nonliquidity traders can choose to be either informed or uninformed. Also, because the analysis is conducted within a rational-expectations framework, the uninformed traders partially infer the knowledge of the informed traders by observing equilibrium prices. Miller and Copeland also state the conditions under which welfare is improved by additional public disclosure requirements: Public information reduces the variance of the price random variable, leads to a more efficient distribution of the risky asset after trading, and satisfies the Kaldor-Hicks-Scitovsky compensation test. Although the analytical assumptions underlying the theorems producing this result are restrictive, Miller and Copeland demonstrate by numerical simulations that the same conclusions apply to more interesting cases.

Although other analyses of public information disclosure could be employed to reach different conclusions, the authors' choice to model disclosure requirements as reduction of the cost of information is intuitively appealing. Others (such as Diamond, 1985)[2] model disclosure as a release of public information that augments information of both informed and uninformed traders. However, in the context of accounting disclosure regulation, it is hard to conceive of a regulatory demand for disclosure that does not stem from lobbying by private-sector groups that would have expended resources to acquire the information privately were they unable to secure mandatory disclosure. Thus, a scenario whereby public disclosure provides information incremental to what a nonman-

Market,'' in *The Proceedings of the Sixth International Conference on Accounting Education,* Japan Accounting Association, 1988.

2. D. Diamond, ''Optimal Release of Information by Firms,'' *Journal of Finance* 40 (1985), pp. 1071–1094.

datory disclosure regime would yield is not as plausible as the scenario analyzed by the authors. And, notwithstanding the fact that Miller and Copeland ignore production effects of information (which are likely to further increase the welfare effects of public information disclosure), the implications of their analysis for the globalization of financial information point with little ambiguity to enhanced public disclosure. In today's world, where the most unveiling is done by U.S. corporations, accounting harmonization along U.S. standards and regulations would seem to be coincident with enhanced public disclosure and, hence, welfare.

Suppose that the welfare improvements posited by Miller and Copeland materialize upon harmonization and enhanced disclosure. Could anything be said about how such welfare gains are distributed among investors in securities and issuers of securities in the different countries? Albeit constrained by the quest for tractability in their modeling, Branson and Jaffee give us an intriguing glimpse into the directions in which research in this area can eventually lead us. Their paper demonstrates both the richness and the complexities of the implications of informational quality changes across countries for such empirically observable manifestations as home asset preferences (the portfolio share allocated to the foreign assets is higher for foreign investors) and security risk premiums. The differences in the implications depend not only on the nature of the information improvement, but also on the locus of information access. Further, there typically will be both gainers and losers in the information improvement game. Although the paper's critic, Michael Adler, exhorts: ''The effects of changes in the quality of information are going to be hard to isolate, quite aside from their being theoretically indeterminant,'' it is rather tempting to follow in Branson and Jaffee's custom-chartered path to consider what might happen if, for example, an improvement in information reduces the variance of the return on a foreign asset (while keeping off-diagonal elements in the variance/covariance matrix constant). The results are complex and variable. First, suppose that the reduced risk of the foreign asset is equally transparent to both home and foreign investors; then a larger share of all portfolios would be allocated to the foreign asset, resulting in a reduced foreign asset risk premium. The size of the increased demand of home and foreign investors is proportional to the portfolio shares initially allocated to the foreign asset, and, if home asset preference is initially zero, then home asset preferences would not be affected, whereas if home asset preference is initially positive, it will rise with improvement in foreign asset information. Second, suppose only home investors have access to the improved foreign asset information (such as when better European securities information becomes available to non-European investors); result: only home investors increase their portfolio share of the foreign asset, foreign asset risk premiums will fall, and home asset preference decreases. Third, suppose home and foreign investors each receive improved information on their own respective assets: home investor demands would shift toward the home asset and foreign investor demand would shift toward the foreign asset; thus, home asset preference increases.

In light of the above, consider for example the impending European harmonization in 1992. If Europe's investors perceive a decline in the riskiness of European assets, both U.S. investors and European issuers of securities would gain as a result of the reduced risk premiums of the European securities. But U.S. investors would also face lower expected returns on the European securities. The net gains and losses would be difficult to gauge in the face of these complexities. European investors, for example, will earn lower returns on their local investments as risk premiums on European securities fall and thus will lose some of the excess returns they had earned because of their informational advantage. These subtleties and a few others (such as selective informational improvement pertaining to only certain classes of foreign securities) are amply elaborated on by Branson and Jaffee. By introducing analyses of informational quality changes and the implication of these for capital flows and international investments into the literature, they are likely to instigate future research that will attempt to map the multifaceted effects of the interactions of the information with other aspects of capital flows.

Whereas some restrictive assumptions yielded positive implications of informational improvements for welfare, the analysis in the more general setting of Adler and Prasad introduces a large dose of uncertainty regarding the benefits of information. As these authors state, although globalization of accounting standards and disclosures is likely to provide investors with more information, this need not immediately translate to better information in the sense of improving the forecasting of performance. They find that completely specified asset demand models cannot unambiguously predict how individuals will respond to better information that is publicly available. The particular context in which Adler and Prasad conduct their analysis is the demand for hedging of foreign currencies by investors with foreign holdings who may wish to reduce their exposure to foreign currency fluctuations. Empirical observations in previous studies suggest that whereas the risk premium on foreign currency converges to zero in the long run, it is mean-reverting in the short run. The behavior of the forward risk premium (the mean change in future prices) is modeled as an exogenous zero-mean-reverting diffusion process. Investors estimate the risk premium based on their prior beliefs and the observed changes in currency prices, and they update these estimates continuously. Hedging of foreign currencies in this model depends on these estimates and their precision.

Adler and Prasad show that when the forecasting power of a certain currency increases (i.e., when investors' previous forecasts are closer to actual changes in prices), the demand for hedging that currency is reduced (this is intuitively plausible since hedging demand is partially due to uncertainty about the evolution of the risk premium) but speculative demand for forward exchange contracts is unaffected. They also show that when investors' forecasting precision increases (i.e., when the *ex ante* forecast variance decreases, hedging demand decreases and speculative demand increases).

These propositions can be tied to changes in information regarding a specific currency or all currencies. When more information and, hence, better predictions are available about a given currency, hedging demand for the currencies decreases, but speculative demand may actually increase. However, more information per se does not guarantee improved predictions: Unless forecasting precision is enhanced, additional information may not be socially desirable.

Does all this ambiguity cast doubt on the desirability of globalization of information and hence the expansion of the total set of disclosed information worldwide? Adler and Prasad proffer two arguments suggesting this is not the case. First, globalization of information would help remove information asymmetries. Second, uniform global financial reporting and disclosure standards would likely contribute to the precision of equity analysis and, more importantly, to the ability of owners to monitor managers: an unambiguous benefit.

Peering into this labyrinth of analytical subtleties of the papers just described, we conclude that on balance, considering the production effects of information and its role in the mitigation of informational asymmetries and moral hazard, the globalization and harmonization of accounting standards and disclosure rules probably enhances welfare. This conclusion is of course predicated on the plausible premise that global information, once produced and disseminated, is indeed acted upon by world markets' participants. Is there a corroborating evidence? Does the availability of information about the markets of one country affect traders' behavior in another? One of the two empirical papers included in this volume demonstrates that this is indeed the case.

Geman, Savanayana, and Schneeweis compare the price variability of futures contracts on the governmental bonds in France during trading and nontrading hours. Previous studies in the United States show that price variability during trading hours is larger than price variability during nontrading hours. In contrast, Geman, Savanayana, and Schneeweis find that the price variability is greater in nontrading hours on the Matif (the French exchange) than in trading hours. This is attributed to the arrival of important foreign information during nontrading hours in France (but trading hours in the United States and Japan).

Geman, Savanayana and Schneeweis also examine the effects of particular local information on price variability. They show that on days when important local macroeconomic information (e.g., money supply) is disclosed, the price variability during trading hours is approximately the same as that of nontrading hours. The combined evidence suggests that both local and foreign information affect the variability of prices in the local market.

The other empirical paper in this issue, that by Darrough and Harris, addresses a different issue. If information globalization and harmonization is to be effected, what sets of information should be globally disclosed in a systematic fashion? After all, if information is disclosed in the United States that is not disclosed elsewhere, we would like to ascertain that indeed the U.S. disclosure has an impact on traders' behavior and, furthermore, that if that information were to be disclosed in other countries, it would in turn impact traders' behavior in those other countries as well as in the United States. In other words, do U.S. disclosures that affect the U.S. market have similar effects on traders' behaviors elsewhere when disclosed there? Moreover, does information not disclosed in the United States affect traders' behavior in countries in which it is disclosed?

The Darrough and Harris paper first extends results found in the U.S. markets with respect to the impact of information to Japanese markets. But it also examines the impact in the Japanese market of disclosures not now provided in the United States, namely, mandatory management forecasts of earnings announced simultaneously with the annual earnings. (The announcements are made separately for parents and consolidated earnings.) If disclosures similar to those made in the United States have similar impacts on market manifestations as in the United States and, furthermore, if disclosures incremental to those in the United States, such as mandatory management forecasts, also have effects on traders' behavior in Japan, one is more confident that financial disclosures worldwide would be used to advantage across nations.

As mentioned, Darrough and Harris examine managerial forecasts in Japan and their effects on security prices. Most Japanese firms make these forecasts available to the public, whereas in the United States only a small proportion of firms disclose managerial forecasts.

Darrough and Harris show that, consistent with findings in the United States, investors react to the disclosure of parent-only earnings of firms. Furthermore, investors also react to managerial forecasts of next year's parent-only earnings. Similar but weaker results obtain for consolidated earnings.

These results may indicate the potential importance of managerial forecasts of earnings beyond Japan. The authors conjecture that the observed higher P/E ratios in Japan may be attributed (among other things) to the availability of good forecasts about future earnings. The desirability of requiring managerial forecasts in other countries is also discussed in the study, based on the evidence in Japan.

From all the studies in this volume—the first to address the impact of information quality enhancement on international capital flows and welfare—it is fair to conclude that the analysis, on balance, points to the desirability of globalization and harmonization of accounting standards and disclosures. The empirical investigations, even though only peripherally related to the central issue of the impact of globalization of accounting disclosures, demonstrate the efficacy of increased disclosures worldwide in terms of the impact on market behavior and the efficiency and speed at which information generated and disseminated in one country is diffused to other countries and is manifested in observable market parameters.

The Welfare Effects of Public Information in an Asymmetric Information Market

BRUCE L. MILLER* AND THOMAS E. COPELAND**

1. INTRODUCTION

The consequences of public disclosure requirements are quite complex. Even if we limit our analysis to an exchange economy setting, public disclosure in a capital market would have at least three important effects that should be taken into account:

1. The effect on equilibrium prices and the investment decisions of traders.
2. The effect on the costs of firm compliance with accounting standards.
3. The effect on the costs of private information gathering.

In the U.S. capital market, additional public disclosure requirements would be expected to increase the costs in category (2), but probably decrease the costs in category (3) as analysts and investors take advantage of the newly available information. If we consider the combined effect of (2) and (3), then it is believed that the total costs increased as the result of FASB Statement No. 33 (inflation accounting), whereas the total costs may well have decreased as the result of FASB Statement No. 14 (segment reporting). If we turn our attention to public disclosure in the capital markets of less developed countries or to the harmonization and conformity of international accounting standards, then the analysis of the effect of any requirements on the combined costs in categories (2) and (3) would encounter considerations different from those in the United States. In conclusion, the effects of public disclosure requirements on

*Anderson Graduate School of Management, UCLA.

**Anderson Graduate School of Management, UCLA, and McKinsey and Co., New York.

We wish to thank Franklin Allen, Joel Demski, Nils Hakansson, Arnold Harberger, Wayne Landsman, Baruch Lev, James Ohlson, TaeYoung Paik, Joshua Ronen, Brett Trueman, and participants at Columbia University and UC–Berkeley workshops for helpful discussions and comments on earlier drafts.

categories (2) and (3) are varied and complicated, which leads us to limit our focus.

In this paper we consider the welfare effects of public information on equilibrium prices and the investment decisions of traders (category 1) only. It will be understood, and the reader will occasionally be reminded, that any estimate of the desirability of public disclosure would need to take into account categories (2) and (3) as well as effects that would arise in a more general production setting.[1] However, in many instances of possible additional (or reduced) disclosure requirements, the sign and the order of magnitude of the effect on costs in (2) and (3) would be known, and a handle on category (1) would be welcome.

Beginning with Hirshleifer (1971), the social value of public information in exchange economies has been extensively analyzed. That paper and most of the subsequent literature have also limited their analysis of the effect of public disclosure to category (1). One conclusion of this literature is that information can make everyone worse off by reducing risk-sharing opportunities. This conclusion can be interpreted as public information making endowment wealth risky; hence, Hirshleifer's term *distribution risk*. The concept of distribution risk will be used to interpret some of the results in this paper. A general result on how information can lead to a Pareto inferior equilibrium is Ohlson (1987, proposition 5.18). Another important result is Lemma 3 of Hakansson, Kunkel, and Ohlson (1982), which says that public information cannot increase welfare in a single-period setting using the Pareto criterion if (a) financial markets achieve full allocational efficiency and (b) information structures are homogeneous. However Theorem 1 of that paper shows that if endowments constitute equilibrium allocations without information, then a Pareto improvement can obtain with public information if either (a) or (b) is not satisfied. For a survey and critique of this literature, see Verrecchia (1982b).

This paper considers an asymmetric information model patterned after Grossman and Stiglitz (1980). In our model there are informed traders, uninformed traders, and liquidity traders, and all have exponential utility functions but with varying risk tolerances. The role of public information

---

1. There is intuition that says that including production in the analysis should increase the desirability of public disclosure since such disclosure should help capital find its most efficient use. However, it is difficult to obtain general results on the welfare effects of information in a production setting. For example, any general results should include the results in an exchange economy as a special case.

is to increase the proportion of informed traders. A main result is a theorem showing that public information passes the Kaldor–Hicks–Scitovsky compensation test. This test is discussed in Section 4. In brief, Kaldor, Hicks, and Scitovsky say that a policy change is an improvement if the winners can compensate the losers. Our theorem is obtained under restrictive assumptions, and numerical calculations are made to evaluate more interesting cases with the same conclusion. The intuition for our result has two strands. First, public information mitigates thin markets, which are vulnerable to random shocks (liquidity trading in our model), and it makes the price-random variable less risky (proposition 4). Therefore, the distribution risk for traders with endowments of the risky asset should be smaller with public information. Second, public information leads to a more efficient distribution of the risky asset after trading (proposition 5). It eliminates the discrepancy in the speculative positions taken by informed and uninformed traders.

These positive welfare results contrast with the negative conclusions in many of the previous investigations of the effects of public information in single-period exchange economies. In these previous studies public information is new to all market participants, whereas in this paper we assume that public information is already known to a fraction of the market participants. In Section 5 we consider an alternative model where public information is new to all participants. In this situation the effect on the price random variable and on welfare is ambiguous. An example is given where welfare decreases with public information, and another example is given where it increases.

The intuition behind the formulation of this model and the interpretation of its conclusions are especially influenced by two papers. Lev (1988) argues that informational equity in capital markets can be used as an operational concept to provide insight into disclosure regulation. Informational equity in capital markets is defined as *ex ante* equality of opportunity, and is obtained when all investors are equally endowed with information. Without such equity, Lev notes "the adverse social effects brought about by the defensive measures taken by uninformed investors who perceive significant inequity" (p. 7).[2] An asymmetric information model is needed to capture the effect described by Lev of a trader's being

---

2. The main paper cited by Lev to substantiate this quote is Glosten and Milgrom (1985), which among other contributions generalizes and extends to a dynamic setting the trading model of Copeland and Galai (1983). Glosten and Milgrom show how informational asymmetries can lead to a market closing. However, they do not show that information increases welfare.

less informed and being aware that he is less informed. Furthermore, our model assumes that public information reduces informational inequity. Hakansson (1981) has examined through examples the effects of public disclosure on seven different types of consumer-investors. He shows how some traders will gain and some will lose with various types of disclosure (Table 2, p. 18). Thus, the standard Pareto criterion cannot be applied. Although not as rich as Hakansson's, an important aspect of our model is that we consider heterogeneous traders (varying risk tolerances and implicity varying costs for acquiring and analyzing information) and liquidity traders. Our model also can have winners and losers, and the net effect on traders is evaluated using the compensation test since the standard Pareto criterion is not applicable.

The paper is organized as follows: Section 2 describes the model, and Section 3 considers the equilibrium. In Section 4 a welfare evaluation of public information is made. Section 5 considers an alternative model where public information is new to all traders. Section 6 discusses related asymmetric information models in the literature and possible extensions of this analysis, and Section 7 evaluates the implications of our model for the harmonization of international accounting standards. Section 8 contains some concluding remarks.

2. THE MODEL

Our model is patterned after the asymmmetric information model of Grossman and Stiglitz (1980). We consider a single-period model with trading taking place at date 0 and the payoffs taking place at date 1. There are two assets in the economy: a riskless bond which pays 1 at date 1, and a risky asset which pays

$$(1) \qquad\qquad u = \theta + \epsilon$$

at date 1, where θ and ϵ are independent and normally distributed with a mean and variance of $(\mu_\theta, 1/h)$ and $(0, 1/s)$, respectively. The price at date 0 of the safe asset (the numeraire) is 1, and the price of the risky asset is P.

All traders including liquidity traders have an exponential utility function. The expected utility of wealth of trader t is

$$(2) \qquad\qquad -E(\exp[-W_t/r(t)]),$$

where W_t is the wealth of trader t, E represents expected value, and $r(t)$ is the risk tolerance of trader t. It is desirable that the risk tolerance be allowed to vary to conform with empirical evidence of widely varying risk tolerances in individuals. Nonliquidity traders trade at date 0 so as to maximize (2). Nonliquidity traders are evaluated according to wealth at date 1; liquidity traders are evaluated according to wealth at date 0.

There is a continuum of traders indexed by t over the interval $[0, 1 + \gamma]$, and three types of traders: informed traders, uninformed traders, and liquidity traders.[3] Liquidity traders are described later and are assumed to be inherently of that type. Thus, the proportion of liquidity traders is unaffected by public information. Traders become informed by paying a charge including the opportunity cost for their time, which we can allow to vary from trader to trader since the charges are only considered implicitly in this model. With the exponential utility function, this charge would not affect a trader's portfolio decisions, which are independent of wealth. For our purposes this cost can be assumed to be absorbed into the endowment of bonds. These are the costs described as category (3) costs in the Introduction. In the interesting case of insider information, the cost of becoming informed would be low for insiders but very high for outsiders.

Let λ be the proportion of nonliquidity traders who choose to become informed in the no-public-information case. Thus, without public information the relative fractions of the three types of traders are proportional to their respective interval lengths (the Lebesgue measure), which are λ, $1 - \lambda$, and γ respectively where $0 < \lambda < 1$. With public information the cost of becoming informed is assumed to decrease,[4] and an additional fraction $\lambda^D - \lambda > 0$ of traders are assumed to decide to become informed, where D stands for disclosure. Therefore, this model captures the idea in Lev (1988) that public information can reduce or eliminate the informational inequities in the informational endowments of traders.

Informed traders know the realized value of θ before trading and the distribution of ϵ. Uninformed traders also know the distribution of ϵ, but they do not know the realized value of θ or its distribution, so they use a diffuse prior for θ, that is, a uniform distribution over the real line.[5]

---

3. Allen (1987) also uses these three types of traders. An important simplifying consequence of this formulation is that the nonliquidity traders have no direct knowledge of x, the per capita supply of the risky asset.

4. This idea can be found in Diamond (1985, p. 1088), who writes, "In this view, the beneficial role of disclosure also includes a reduction in such analysts' costs of operation."

5. The assumption of a diffuse prior makes the analysis more tractable. This prior will be combined with the likelihood function of a sample of size one, the price of the risky asset, to yield the posterior distribution of θ. The uniform prior as a representation of ignorance satisfies desirable invariance

Uninformed traders are assumed to have the same reasons that decision makers in general can have for using a diffuse prior.[6] They do know P and the underlying equation and parameters that determine P so that they can use P to make inferences about θ. The equation for P is given in the next section. In Section 5 we consider an alternative model where uninformed traders do have access to the correct prior distribution of θ. Informed traders do not need to use this equation since they have perfect information about θ.

An informed trader or uninformed trader t, $0 \leq t \leq 1$, is endowed with $\bar{B}(t)$ bonds (possibly adjusted to reflect an information-gathering charge) and $e(t)$ risky assets. At date 0 trader t buys $B(t)$ bonds and X_t risky assets subject to a budget constraint:

$$(3) \qquad W_{0t} = \bar{B}(t) + e(t)P = B(t) + X_t P.$$

At date 1 trader t's wealth is $W_{1t} = B(t) + X_t u$.

Liquidity traders are assumed to trade on the basis of information orthogonal to the value of the risky asset.[7] Life-cycle trading is an example often given of liquidity trading. A desirable property of a market is that

properties for a normally distributed sample with a known variance (Villegas, 1977, p. 454) and Hartigan (1964, p. 844). An uninformed trader's prior knowledge would be expected to lie between the extremes of a diffuse prior and the correct prior. A justification for choosing the lower bound is that although our model underestimates an uninformed trader's prior information, it (and other models as well) overestimates his ability to learn from the price of the risky asset since it overlooks the issue of estimating the underlying equation and parameters that determine P.

6. Cyert and DeGroot (1987, p. 19) write, "In some problems, the prior information of the DM (decision maker) about the parameter Θ is vague relative to the information about Θ that will be obtained by observing X. . . . Also, because the DM will soon acquire relatively precise information about Θ from the observation X, it will typically not be worthwhile for the DM to spend much time making a careful determination of the prior distribution. In this type of situation it may be convenient to use a standard prior distribution that is suitable as an approximate representation of vague prior information. The standard prior distribution that is used is often an *improper distribution* in the sense that it is represented by a nonnegative density for which the integral over the entire space Ω is infinite rather than 1." It may be helpful to contrast our assumption that uninformed traders have vague prior information about θ with the assumption that they know the distribution of ϵ. The random variable ϵ represents the error term of an informed trader's estimate of the payoff u, and its distribution is described by one parameter, the variance. The random variable θ is the value of the payoff u less the error term ϵ, and its distribution is described by two parameters, a mean and a variance. Our assumption is that uninformed traders have a good idea of the reliability of informed traders' forecasts, but are unable and/or unwilling to make forecasts *themselves* that are informative.

7. Without uncertainty in the supply of the risky asset, price fully reveals information (see proposition 3 below). As Verrecchia (1982a) points out, full revelation can be objected to on empirical grounds. Liquidity traders are needed to model shocks that are not related to the value of the risky asset.

it is liquid, and that a trader will not be greatly harmed by buying or selling on short notice (see, for example, Lippman and McCall, 1986). In our model, liquidity traders rely on price to be a good guide to value and implicitly are assumed to be price inelastic.

Liquidity trader t, $1 < t \leq 1 + \gamma$, does not maximize but simply sells $e(t) + (1/\gamma)(x - \bar{e})$ of risky assets at date 0, where $e(t)$ is a scalar, and the normally distributed random variable x has a mean of $\bar{e}$ and a variance of V.[8] Of course, a negative quantity sold is interpreted as a purchase. The mean $\bar{e}$ is set equal to $\int_0^{1+\gamma} e(t)dt$ so that x represents the per capita (exclusive of liquidity traders) supply. The random variables x, ϵ, and θ are independent. At date 0 liquidity trader t's wealth is $(e(t) + (1/\gamma)(x - \bar{e}))P$.[9] The expected utility of liquidity traders is measured at date 0. At date 1 liquidity trader t receives a payoff of $-(e(t) + (1/\gamma)(x - \bar{e}))u$, but this is not included in the analysis since it does not vary with public information.

Having developed some of our notation, we review the sequence of events. At date 0 before trading, a fraction λ or λ^D (the public disclosure case) of the traders become informed and the random variables θ and x are realized. Then the equilibrium price P is determined and trading takes place. Subsequently, the random variable ϵ is realized, and the payoffs from the bond and the risky asset are received at date 1.

Our model has four important differences from that of Grossman and Stiglitz (1980). First, uninformed traders use a diffuse prior for θ in our model. Second, in our model the cost of becoming informed is modeled implicitly. Thus, at no additional complexity we can assume that this cost varies among traders. Third, we allow traders to have different risk tolerances. Fourth, we introduce liquidity traders who take the place of the random endowments of informed and uninformed traders in Grossman and Stiglitz.

---

8. Most if not all of our results would still hold if we add a random amount $y(t)$ to liquidity trader t's endowment where $y(t)$ is a normally distributed random variable with mean 0 and variance Y. The $y(t)$ would be assumed to be independent so in the spirit of the strong law of large numbers

$$\int_1^{1+\gamma} y(t)dt = 0 \text{ almost surely}$$

as in Laffont (1985, note 5). Also see Judd (1985).

9. Thus, wealth is the receipt (or cost) from the sale (or purchase) of the risky assets at date 0, and it does not include other assets the liquidity trader may have. Allen (1987) also evaluates liquidity trader wealth by this method.

3. THE EQUILIBRIUM

The focus of this section is to evaluate the expected value of wealth of traders at date 1 conditioned on θ and x. By the assumptions of the model, W_{1t} is normally distributed so that we can calculate the desired expected utility using the formula for the moment-generating function of the normal distribution. As in Grossman and Stiglitz (1980, eq. (7)), for nonliquidity traders

(4) $-E(\exp[-W_{1t}/r(t)|X_t,\theta,x]) = -\exp[-(W_{0t}/r(t) + X_t(\theta - P)/r(t)$
$$- (X_t^2/2r(t)^2)(1/s))],$$

where X_t is the amount of risky assets purchased at date 0 and is not assumed to have any optimality properties. Each informed trader knows θ and P and sets X_t equal to X_{It} where

(5) $X_{It} = r(t)s(\theta - P).$

This is the familiar result that a trader's demand with the exponential utility function does not depend on wealth. Recall that uninformed traders know only P. As in Grossman and Stiglitz eq. (7'), an uninformed trader t sets X_t equal to X_{Ut} so as to maximize

(6) $\begin{aligned} &-\exp[-(W_{0t}/r(t) + X_{Ut}(E[u|P] - P)/r(t) - \\ &(X_{Ut}^2/2r(t)^2)\mathrm{Var}[u|P])]. \end{aligned}$

The maximizing value of X_{Ut} is

(7) $X_{Ut} = r(t)(E[u|P] - P)/\mathrm{Var}[u|P].$

In equilibrium, P must be such that

(8) $X_I + X_U = x,$

where X_I is the demand of the informed traders and equals $r_1 s(\theta - P)$, and X_U is the demand of the uninformed traders and equals $(r - r_1)(E[u|P] - P)/\mathrm{var}[u|P]$. The parameter $r_1 = \int_0^\lambda r(t)dt$, and $r = \int_0^1 r(t)dt$. In the case of public information we substitute $r_1^D = \int_0^{\lambda^D} r(t)dt$ for r_1. We temporarily assume that $\lambda^D < 1$. The case where $\lambda^D = 1$ is described after proposition 2 and causes no complications.

Grossman and Stiglitz show that the random price P is influenced by the distribution of θ only through the beliefs of the uninformed about θ. Therefore, we conjecture and prove that the solution for P in our model is the limit of their solution as the variance of the prior of θ goes to infinity. We give this limit as proposition 1. All proofs are given in the Appendix.

Proposition 1. The limit of the price function in the Grossman–Stiglitz model as the variance of the prior of θ goes to infinity is

$$(9) \qquad P = \omega_\lambda - \bar{e}/(r_1 s + (r - r_1)/(1/s + (1/r_1 s)^2 V)),$$

where

$$(10) \qquad \omega_\lambda = \theta - (x - \bar{e})/r_1 s.$$

We next show that the price P in proposition 1 does equate supply and demand in our model, and at the same time we establish the quantity of risky assets purchased by informed and uninformed traders.

Proposition 2. The price P in proposition 1 is the equilibrium price function. Also,

$$(11) \qquad X_{It} = (r(t)/r_1)(x - \delta\bar{e}), \text{ and}$$

$$(12) \qquad X_{Ut} = (r(t)/(r - r_1))\delta\bar{e},$$

where

$$(13) \quad \delta = ((r - r_1)/(1/s + (1/r_1 s)^2 V))/(r_1 s + (r - r_1)/(1/s + (1/r_1 s)^2 V)).$$

It follows from proposition 2 that uninformed traders purchase $X_U = \delta\bar{e}$ of the risky asset, whereas the informed traders purchase $X_I = (1 - \delta)\bar{e} + (x - \bar{e})$ of the risky asset. Clearly the equilibrium condition (8) is satisfied. The equations in this section were derived for $0 < \lambda < 1$. For $\lambda^D = 1$ they hold with the following modification. The equations for the uninformed traders are eliminated, and r_1 becomes r and δ equals 0.

We now confirm that if the supply of the securities is nonrandom, then uninformed traders will make the same decisions as the informed traders as price fully reveals information. This holds despite their use of a diffuse prior. If $V = 0$, then $\delta = (r - r_1)/r$ and $x = \bar{e}$. Direct substitution for δ and x yields:

Proposition 3. If $V = 0$, then $X_{It} = X_{Ut} = r(t)\bar{e}/r$.

It will be helpful to obtain a compact expression for $\theta - P$, which is used in (4). From the definition of δ,

$$1 - \delta = r_1 s/(r_1 s + (r - r_1)/(1/s + (1/r_1 s)^2 V)).$$

Substituting $1 - \delta$ into (9) yields

$$P = \omega_\lambda - (1 - \delta)\bar{e}/r_1 s,$$

which can be rearranged, using (10), as

(14) $$\theta - P = (x - \delta\bar{e})/r_1 s.$$

Let $V_{It}(\theta,x) = -E(\exp[-W_{1t}/r(t)|X_{It},\theta,x])$ be the expected utility of an informed trader t conditioned on θ and x. Similarly, let $V_{Ut}(\theta,x) = -E(\exp[-W_{1t}/r(t)|X_{Ut},\theta,x])$ be the expected utility of an uninformed trader t conditioned on θ and x. Substituting into (4), letting $X_t = X_{It}$, and using (3), (11), and (14) yields

(15) $$V_{It}(\theta,x) = -\exp[-((\bar{B}(t) + e(t)P)/r(t) + (1/2r_1^2 s)(x - \delta\bar{e})^2)].$$

Substituting into (4), letting $X_t = X_{Ut}$, and using (3), (12), and (14) yields

(16) $$V_{Ut}(\theta,x) = -\exp[-((\bar{B}(t) + e(t)P)/r(t) + (\delta\bar{e}/(r - r_1)r_1 s)(x - \delta\bar{e}) - (\delta\bar{e})^2/(2(r - r_1)^2 s))].$$

Finally, let $V_{Lt}(\theta,x)$ be the expected utility of a liquidity trader t conditioned on θ and x, and recall that liquidity trader t's wealth equals $(e(t) + (1/\gamma)(x - \bar{e}))P$. By (14),

(17) $$V_{Lt}(\theta,x) = -\exp[-((e(t) - \bar{e}/\gamma)P + (x/\gamma)(\theta - (x - \delta\bar{e})/r_1 s))/r(t)].$$

Because of the positive coefficient of the x^2 term in the exponent, there are parameters such that the (unconditional) expected utility of a liquidity trader can be minus infinity. To rule out this implausible situation, we assume that for $1 < t \le 1 + \gamma$, $r(t)$ is sufficiently large that

(18) $$V_{Lt} > -\infty,$$

where V_{Lt} is the expected utility of liquidity trader t.

Before analyzing the welfare effects of public information, we consider how public information affects the price-random variable P. The following proposition shows that public information can mitigate the price instability of markets.

Proposition 4. The variance of P decreases with public information.

The intuition for this result is that the demand for risky assets is elastic for informed traders (see (5)) but inelastic for uninformed traders (see (12) and (13)), and public information increases the fraction of informed traders. The supply of risky assets with or without public information is inelastic but random.

Proposition 4 is important for understanding how public information can lead to a welfare improvement. To see why we obtain a welfare improvement while Hirshleifer (1971) does not, let us review some important features of the Hirshleifer model. He considers a public information system that reveals a signal before trading. With public information there is a different equilibrium (and price) associated with each possible signal, whereas without public information there is only one equilibrium and hence price is not random. In our model there is a different equilibrium associated with each value of θ and x, with or without public information. By proposition 4 the price of the risky asset is, in fact, more volatile without public information.

4. WELFARE EFFECTS OF PUBLIC INFORMATION

4.1. The Kaldor–Hicks–Scitovsky Compensation Test

A major topic in welfare economics is developing criteria for preferring equilibrium A to equilibrium B. If everyone is at least as well off in equilibrium A as in equilibrium B, and some are better off (the Pareto criterion), then there is general agreement that A is preferred to B. But what if some individuals prefer A and others prefer B? As described in Mansfield (1985, Chapter 15), there are two prominent approaches in this situation. The first approach is to define an explicit social welfare function. The Mirrlees (1971) paper on optimal individual income tax rates adopts this approach. The second approach is to use the Kaldor–Hicks–Scitovsky compensation test, and this is the approach we take. The Grossman and Hart (1981, p. 263) paper on takeover bids uses the second approach. Both of these tests are weaker than the Pareto criterion, but they have a greater domain of applicability. See Sen (1970) for an authoritative discussion of these and other welfare criteria.

The Kaldor–Hicks–Scitovsky compensation test says that equilibrium A is preferred to equilibrium B if there is a zero sum set of transfer payments that transforms A to A' and A' is Pareto preferred to B, and that there is no zero sum set of transfer payments that transforms B to B' and B' is Pareto preferred to A. It is not anticipated that the zero sum set of transfer payments would be made in any particular case. Harberger's (1971) postulates for applied welfare economics are along the lines of this compensation test. His third postulate states, "When evaluating the net benefits or costs of a given action (project, program, or policy), the costs and benefits accruing to each member of the relevant group (e.g., a nation) should normally be added without regard to the individual(s) to whom they accrue." In fact, the Kaldor–Hicks–Scitovsky compensation test is the primary justification for the use of cost–benefit analysis in the public domain, and Broadway (1974) points out some of the difficulties in demonstrating that cost–benefit analyses satisfy the compensation test.

The compensation test is an efficiency test, and, for example, in a deterministic single good economy with production it is easy to see that the equilibrium with the higher aggregate output will be the preferred. However, the compensation test is open to the criticism that it neglects the redistribution effects of a move from one equilibrium to another (Little, 1957, Chapter 6). Hicks (1941, p. 111) attempts to overcome this criticism by arguing that consistent application of this criterion would lead to "a strong possibility that almost all [individuals] would be better off after the lapse of a sufficient length of time." See Small (1987) for recent results substantiating Hicks' belief. Another response to this criticism is to take into account redistribution effects, as in the proposal by Ng (1984) to require that the compensation test be satisfied by each income group.

In summary, the Kaldor–Hicks–Scitovsky compensation test is the main welfare test for an improvement in efficiency, but passing it is not proof of a welfare improvement because of possible adverse redistribution effects. Although we do not attempt an examination of the redistribution effects of public information in our model, we point out that public information is not thought to favor economically advantaged investors.

The following lemma will be useful for showing that public information passes the compensation test.

Lemma 1. Consider a model with a continuum of traders in some interval $[0, Y]$, and suppose that each trader has the exponential utility function (2) of wealth. Let expected utility of wealth for trader t equal $-\exp[-f_A(t)/r(t)]$ in equilibrium A and equal $-\exp[-f_B(t)/r(t)]$ in equilibrium B. Then equilibrium A is preferred to equilibrium B in the sense of Kaldor–Hicks–Scitovsky if

$$\int_0^Y f_A(t) > \int_0^Y f_B(t).$$

Before going on to the main results in the paper, we illustrate the Kaldor–Hicks–Scitovsky compensation test by applying it to a simple financial model with no informational asymmetries.

Example 1. Consider a model with a continuum of traders in the interval $[0, 1]$, and suppose that each trader has the exponential utility function (2) of wealth. Each trader t is endowed with $\bar{B}(t)$ bonds and $e(t)$ risky assets at date 0. The bonds pay 1 at date 1; the risky asset pays u where u is normally distributed with a mean of μ and a variance of σ^2. All traders know the distribution of u. The price of the safe asset is normalized to 1, and the price of the risky asset is P. Trading takes place at date 0 with each trader seeking to maximize her expected utility of date 1 wealth.

The solution approach to the trading equilibrium for this problem is well known. Let $\bar{e} = \int_0^1 e(t)dt$ and $r = \int_0^1 r(t)dt$. Then $P = \mu - (\bar{e}\sigma^2)/r$, and each trader t holds $r(t)\bar{e}/r$ risky assets after trading. The expected utility of each trader t is $-\exp[-f(t)/r(t)]$ where $f(t) = \bar{B}(t) + e(t)P + .5(\bar{e}/r)^2\sigma^2 r(t)$. Therefore,

(19) $$\int_0^1 f(t) = \int_0^1 \bar{B}(t)dt + \bar{e}\mu + \int_0^1 [-(e(t)\bar{e}/r) + .5(\bar{e}/r)^2 r(t)]\sigma^2 dt.$$

Now we consider two equilibriums. In equilibrium A, $\sigma^2 = \sigma_A^2$, and in equilibrium B, $\sigma^2 = \sigma_B^2$, with $\sigma_A^2 < \sigma_B^2$. Is equilibrium A preferred to equilibrium B? Since traders are risk averse, equilibrium A seems preferable in some sense. Trader t will prefer A if and only if $e(t)\bar{e}/r \geq .5(\bar{e}/r)^2 r(t)$. Therefore, A is not, in general, Pareto preferred to B. Traders with "small" endowments of the risky asset and "high" risk tolerances prefer B. However, equilibrium A is preferred to equilibrium B in the sense of Kaldor–Hicks–Scitovsky using Lemma 1 and (19) since

□ $$\int_0^1 f_A(t) - \int_0^1 f_B(t) = -.5[\bar{e}^2/r]\sigma_A^2 + .5[\bar{e}^2/r]\sigma_B^2 > 0.$$

4.2. Analytical Results

We will apply the Kaldor–Hicks–Scitovsky compensation test to public information. The calculations get rather intricate and our proof that public information passes the compensation test requires that $e(t)$ equals 0 for all traders t. Numerical simulations will be resorted to for more general settings without this restriction.

Proposition 4, which says that P is less risky with public information, is one reason we anticipate that public information passes the compensation test. A second reason is that public information leads to a more efficient distribution of risky assets after trading. To show this we consider the situation where we condition on θ and x and note that P is constant on this set. We will find that only the after-trading distribution of risky assets is relevant for the compensation test, and that public information passes the test (proposition 5 below). Although proposition 5 holds for all θ and x, we cannot take expected values and obtain the general result because the transfer payments in proposition 5 vary with θ and x. The proof is for the case where $\lambda^D = 1$; the more general situation $\lambda^D < 1$ is much less tractable and was not analyzed.

Proposition 5. Conditioned on θ and x, public information such that $\lambda^D = 1$ passes the Kaldor–Hicks–Scitovsky compensation test.

The next result, Theorem 1, shows that public information passes the compensation test when $e(t)$ equals 0 for all t. We conjecture, but have not been able to show, that this result is also valid for all nonzero $e(t)$ as well. Before proving Theorem 1 it is necessary to establish the following lemmas. The proof of Lemma 2 is given in the Appendix, and Lemma 3 follows from standard probability theory.

Lemma 2. Let x_1, x_2, and c be strictly positive numbers where $x_1 > x_2$. Then $\ln((c/x_1^2 + 1)x_1 - \ln((c/x_2^2) + 1)x_2 \geq c/x_1 - c/x_2$.

Lemma 3. Let x be a normally distributed random variable with a mean of 0 and a variance of V. Then for scalars t_1 and $t_2 > -1/2V$,

$$E(\exp[-(t_1 x + t_2 x^2)]) = \frac{1}{\sqrt{2t_2 V + 1}} \exp[.5t_1^2/(2t_2 + 1/V)].$$

Theorem 1. Suppose that the nonrandom endowment $e(t)$ equals 0 for all traders t, $0 \leq t \leq 1 + \gamma$. Then public information passes the Kaldor–Hicks–Scitovsky compensation test.

4.3. Numerical Simulations

We calculate several examples to see what happens without the restriction $e(t) = 0$. We will find that the conclusions of proposition 2 and Theorem 1 continue to hold for our three numerical simulations. Our parameter values are chosen so that, with public information, the (monthly) mean and variance of the excess return on the market portfolio are .5% and .4%, respectively, following Ibbotson and Sinquefield (1982).

The variance hypothesis implies that $1/s + (1/rs)^2 V = .004$. Since the

Table 1
Examples with $e(t) \neq 0$

λ	λ^D	Information	$\int_0^\lambda f(t)dt$	$\int_\lambda^1 f(t)dt$	$\int_1^{1+\gamma} f(t)dt$	$\int_0^{1+\gamma} f(t)dt$
.01		No Pub. Inf.	.04060	1.56236	-.02351	1.57945
	1.0	Pub. Inf.	.03903	1.56241	-.02009	1.58135
.1		No Pub. Inf.	.33498	1.26660	-.02041	1.58117
	1.0	Pub. Inf.	.33480	1.26663	-.02009	1.58134
.25		No Pub. Inf.	.68977	.91171	-.02020	1.58128
	1.0	Pub. Inf.	.68970	.91173	-.02009	1.58134

term $(1/rs)^2V$ is quite small, we will set $s = 250$. The mean excess return hypothesis, $E(u) - P \approx .005$, implies, using equations (9) and (A1), that $\bar{e}/r = 1.25$. We normalize μ_θ to 1. Our three simulations have the same parameter values except that λ, the faction of informed traders under no public information, assumes the values .01, .10, and .25. In each case λ^D was set equal to 1.0. The parameter values we used are:

1. $e(t) = 1/(.25 + t)$ for $0 \leq t \leq 1$, and $e(t) = 0$ for $1 < t \leq 1 + \gamma$. Therefore, $\bar{e} = 1.6094$.
2. $r(t) = .8/(.25 + t)$ for $0 \leq t \leq 1$. Therefore, $r = 1.2875$. These values are consistent with the hypothesis that wealthier individuals have higher risk tolerances. We set $r(t) = 1.2875$ for $1 < t \leq 1 + \gamma$.
3. $s = h = 250$, $\mu_\theta = 1$, $\gamma = .5$, and $V = .0259$. V was chosen so that the probability that x, the per capita supply of stock, is negative is infinitesimal.

For each trader t we calculated her expected utility as $-\exp[-f(t)/r(t)]$ in order to be able to apply Lemma 1. Some of the equations used in the calculation of Table 1 are given in the Appendix.

The most important column in Table 1 is the last which shows, using Lemma 1, that public information satisfies the Kaldor–Hicks–Scitovsky compensation test. The smaller the proportion of informed traders with no public information, the greater is the margin that public information passes the test. It is noteworthy, but not surprising, that in each example traders who are informed without public information do worse when public information results in more traders' becoming informed. Traders who were previously uninformed do better when public information results in their becoming informed, and liquidity traders definitely prefer public information. The negative entries in the next-to-last column are explained by the zero expected number of shares sold by liquidity traders, their risk aversion, and the negative correlation of price and supply.

Could any simulation show that public information does not pass the compensation test? This question is equivalent to asking if Theorem 1 is valid for all $e(t)$. Our conjecture is that Theorem 1 is valid for all $e(t)$ or, equivalently, that there is no simulation that would show a decrease in welfare using the Kaldor–Hicks–Scitovsky criterion.

5. AN ALTERNATIVE MODEL

Our alternative model makes only one different assumption from the basic model. It assumes that uninformed traders have access to the correct priors. We consider one particular comparison only: We assume that λ, the fraction of informed traders without public information, is 0, and that λ^D, the fraction of informed traders with public information, is 1. This comparison is of special interest because when $\lambda = 0$, public information does bring new information to the market. Without public information, no traders know the value of θ.

5.1. Allen's Results

As part of his analysis Allen (1987) examined precisely this comparison. He obtained the following result:

Proposition 6 (Allen). Suppose that uninformed traders have access to the correct prior of θ, and that λ, the fraction of informed traders without public information, is 0, and that λ^D, the fraction of informed traders with public information, is 1. Then all nonliquidity traders prefer no public information to public information.

Note that proposition 6 does not require that $e(t) = 0$. The hypothesis that $\lambda = 0$ means that public information does not eliminate informational endowment inequities, but simply makes all nonliquidity traders better informed. Although proposition 6 seems to be at odds with our positive results, it is not surprising if we look at our numerical simulations and note that nonliquidity traders taken together are better off without public information. It is the liquidity traders who enable public information to pass the compensation test.

Allen also evaluated the expected utilities of liquidity traders, but he assumed that they were risk-neutral. Liquidity traders gained from public information except when their nonrandom endowments were sufficiently negative.

5.2. The Compensation Test

We examine the effect of public information in this situation using the compensation test. The equations to evaluate expected utility are already in place for public information since priors are irrelevant when $\lambda^D = 1.0$. However, for the no-public-information case, which assumes that $\lambda = 0$ and uninformed traders have correct priors, we need to refer to some additional results.

From equation (A7) in Grossman–Stiglitz, the equilibrium price function when $\lambda = 0$ and uninformed traders have correct priors is

$$(20) \qquad P = \mu_\theta - (x/r)(1/s + 1/h).$$

The effects of the prior information of the uninformed traders is reflected by μ_θ and $1/h$, the mean and variance respectively of the prior of θ, in (20). This is a qualitatively different situation from the price equation (9) where uninformed traders do not "bring" anything to the price function. By (A6) in Grossman–Stiglitz, the uninformed traders purchase $r(t)x/r$ of risky assets.

In the case of public information ($\lambda^D = 1$), our price equation (9) can be written as

$$(21) \qquad P = \theta - x/rs.$$

By (11) we know that the informed traders purchase $r(t)x/r$ of risky assets, the same strategy as the uninformed traders in the no-public-information situation.

We have seen that much of the intuition on whether there is an improvement in welfare from public information can be gleaned from the variance of the price function. Unlike proposition 4, which showed that public information reduced the variance of the price-random variable, the comparison between (20) and (21) is ambiguous. On the one hand the variance of $(x/r)(1/s + 1/h)$ is greater than the variance of x/rs. However, the variance of θ is greater than 0, the variance of the constant μ_θ. Therefore, our next result should not be surprising.

Proposition 7. Suppose that uninformed traders have access to the correct prior of θ, and that λ, the fraction of informed traders without public information, is 0, and that λ^D, the fraction of informed traders with public information, is 1. Then for some parameters public information satisfies the Kaldor–Hicks–Scitovsky compensation test, whereas for others it does not. These sets of parameters can be chosen to satisfy the conditions of Theorem 1.

The proof of proposition 7 is given in the Appendix with the rest of the proofs. The example where public information does not pass the test is constructed from the example where it does pass by, increasing r. Note that as r increases to ∞, $P = \theta$ with public information and $P = \mu_\theta$ without public information. Thus, price is not random without public information. This is the same situation found in Hirshleifer (1971). Recall that he considers a public information system that reveals a signal before trading. With public information there is a different equilibrium (and price) associated with each possible signal, whereas without public information there is only one equilibrium and hence price is not random.

6. RELATED ASYMMETRIC INFORMATION MODELS

In this section we briefly describe asymmetric information models that consider welfare effects and contrast their conclusions with ours. We also suggest future research topics. The Allen (1987) paper cited in the previous section considers the welfare effects of public information in an asymmetric information market, and also uses the Grossman–Stiglitz model of a financial market. Besides the result cited as proposition 6 in the previous section, Allen also looks at a more complex setting where traders can choose to become informed at a price. This formulation requires the assumption that the risk tolerance $r(t)$ does not vary with t. He describes his conclusion as consistent with Hirshleifer (1971) in that information can make everybody worse off.

Diamond (1985) and Indjejikian (1988) analyze the welfare effects of voluntary firm disclosure. If firm disclosure is interpreted as being required, then these two studies also analyze the effect of public disclosure. Diamond bases his financial market on the Verrecchia–Helwig formulation where a trader can receive information at a cost. The information signal is $y_t = u + \epsilon_t$, where the ϵ_t are independent from trader to trader, and u represents the payoff of the risky asset. His formulation also requires that $r(t)$ does not vary with t. Public information is a release of information that, in effect, makes everyone's prior about u more informative. Diamond shows that the more informative prior can result in fewer traders choosing to become informed, and an increase in the welfare of the nonliquidity traders. If public information does not reduce the number of traders who pay to become informed, then the welfare of nonliquidity traders is reduced, and Diamond describes this conclusion as consistent with Hirshleifer.

Indjejikian bases his analysis on a new formulation of a financial market. Each trader receives an information signal $y_t = u + \eta + \epsilon_t$, where η is common noise and ϵ_t is independent from trader to trader with a variance that depends on the cost incurred by the trader to process the information. Public information would have the effect of reducing the variance of η. As in Diamond, Indjejikian only considers the welfare of nonliquidity traders. We do not attempt to summarize his extensive results, which show public information both increasing and decreasing the welfare of nonliquidity traders under various circumstances.

The conclusions of the Allen, Diamond, and Indjejikian models on the welfare effect of public disclosure have a different tenor from our positive conclusion in Theorem 1 or mixed conclusion in proposition 7. Indeed, Allen and Diamond suggest that a tax on information gathering, if it were practical to apply, would be a good thing. Although all the models differ in a number of ways, there are two major differences: The first is whether the welfare of liquidity traders is included in the analysis. Allen includes liquidity traders, but gives them secondary status and assumes that they are risk-neutral; Diamond and Indjejikian do not include them. From Table 1 we see that had we not included liquidity traders in the compensation test, we would have concluded that public information was not desirable in those examples. The second major difference between our model and the other three is that they explicitly include the costs of private information gathering in their welfare analysis.

One topic for future research would be to reconsider the Diamond and Indjejikian models and include liquidity traders and perhaps the compensation test in the analysis. Another would be to find an alternative way to model liquidity traders. They are assumed to precommit to a certain volume of transactions. If the price is unfavorable, it shows up in the welfare analysis by an adverse effect on the liquidity traders. A more realistic model would allow some discretion by liquidity traders. A final topic would have application in the analysis of international markets and is described in the next section.

7. HARMONIZATION OF INTERNATIONAL ACCOUNTING STANDARDS

In this section we consider the harmonization and conformity of international accounting standards. We follow the framework used in the Introduction and consider the possible effect of the harmonization of international accounting standards in three categories—the effect on equilibrium prices and the investment decisions of traders, the effect on the costs of firm compliance with accounting standards, and the effect on the costs of private information gathering. The results of this study are only relevant to the first category as we hope that we have made clear, but we will take this opportunity to briefly state our views on the other two categories and to consider the form that international harmonization might take.

The conclusion of this paper is that public information can improve welfare by mitigating thin markets, which are vulnerable to random shocks, and by eliminating the discrepancy in the speculative positions taken by informed and uninformed traders. Therefore, the harmonization of international accounting, to the extent that it plays the role of public information in our model and leads to a higher fraction of informed traders, improves welfare. Branson and Jaffee (elsewhere in this book) consider a model where there are two risky assets—one domestic and one foreign—and two representative investors—domestic and foreign—who hold portfolios of both assets. The domestic investor is better informed about the domestic investment opportunity. They consider the case where information about the foreign investment improves, the situation corresponding to the harmonization of international accounting standards. One future research topic would be to reconsider their interesting setting using the methodology of this paper.

The welfare effects of disclosure in a non-U.S. setting is explored by Lee (1987). He, too, says that information can benefit capital markets and argues that lack of accounting information hampers the efficiency of capital markets in newly industrialized economies. He presents data on the relative thinness of the Taiwan capital market relative to that of the United States and ties this to the differences between the public disclosure requirements of the two countries.

It is the third category of effects where the appeal of international conformity is strongest. The costs of private information gathering by traders wanting to invest in international markets would drop with international harmonization. However, the costs of firm compliance could be significant in countries where there would be a major departure from current accounting practice.

When we turn to the form that international harmonization might take, some ideas on accounting in Ross (1983) and Wilson (1983) are worth remembering. Ross (p. 380) notes that accounting serves the role of monitoring performance and veracity as well as information for use by capital markets. Wilson (Section 4) argues that accounting boards such as the FASB "serve the collective interest of the profession in designing and coordinating innovations in the language of financial accounting."

The benefit that Wilson sees in the role of the FASB in the United States would also apply to international conformity. As the international markets for securities grow, the attractiveness of a common language of financial accounting increases. Extrapolating from the ideas of Ross, the monitoring and veracity role of accounting information is perhaps best left to individual countries. We speculate that international conformity should take the form of required supplementary information in the notes to the financial statements along with continued efforts to obtain harmonization of the financial statements across nations. Finally, we caution that the decision-making process for implementing international harmonization could be cumbersome. There is a danger that its pronouncements would evolve too slowly.

8. SUMMARY AND CONCLUSION

We have considered a variation of the asymmetric information model of Grossman and Stiglitz. Public information is assumed to increase the proportion of informed traders, so our model incorporates the idea in Lev that public information can reduce or eliminate inequities in the informational endowments of traders. We restrict our analysis to the effect of public information on equilibrium prices and the investment decisions of traders. We find that public information reduces the variance of the price-random variable, leads to a more efficient distribution of the risky asset after trading, and satisfies the Kaldor–Hicks–Scitovsky compensation test. The result on the compensation test is obtained under restrictive assumptions, and numerical calculations are made to evaluate more interesting cases with the same conclusion.

The positive welfare results in this paper contrast with the negative conclusions of many of the previous investigations of the effects of public information in single-period exchange economies with no private information acquisition. There are two properties of our model that could explain our positive welfare results. First, even without public information a positive fraction of the market is assumed to be informed, whereas public information is assumed to be new to all market participants in Hirshleifer and related models. Second, we assume that uninformed traders have diffuse priors rather than access to correct priors. Proposition 7 shows that without these two properties, public information may or may not pass the compensation test.

The conclusions of the asymmetric information models of Allen, Diamond, and Indjejikian also have a different tenor from our positive results on the effect of public information. Although all the models differ in a number of ways, there are two major differences. The first is whether the welfare of liquidity traders is included in the analysis. Allen includes liquidity traders, but gives them secondary status and assumes that they are risk-neutral; Diamond and Indjejikian do not include them. The second major difference between our model and the other three is that they explicitly include the costs of private information gathering in their welfare analysis.

The results in this paper imply that the harmonization of international accounting, to the extent that it plays the role of public information in our model and leads to a higher fraction of informed traders, improves welfare. A future research topic would be to employ the approach of this paper on the model of Branson and Jaffee, who consider two risky assets—one domestic and one foreign—and two representative investors—domestic and foreign—who hold portfolios of both assets.

APPENDIX

Proof of Proposition 1. In our notation, (A10) in Grossman and Stiglitz is,

$$P = \frac{r_1 s w_\lambda + ((r - r_1)/\text{Var}(u|w_\lambda))E(u|w_\lambda) - \bar{e}}{r_1 s + ((r - r_1)/\text{Var}(u|w_\lambda))},$$

where

$$E(u|w_\lambda) = (1/h/(1/h + (1/r_1 s)^2 V))w_\lambda + ((1/r_1 s)^2 V/(1/h + (1/r_1 s)^2 V))\mu_\theta, \text{ and}$$

$$\text{Var}(u|w_\lambda) = 1/h + 1/s - (1/h)^2/(1/h + (1/r_1 s)^2 V).$$

It is clear that $\lim_{h \to 0} E(u|w_\lambda) = w_\lambda$. By writing $\text{Var}(u|w_\lambda)$ as

$$1/s + (1/h(1/h + (1/r_1 s)^2 V) - (1/h)^2)/(1/h + (1/r_1 s)^2 V),$$

it follows that $\lim_{h \to 0} \mathrm{Var}(u|w_\lambda) = 1/s + (1/r_1 s)^2 V$. Substituting these limits into the equation for P completes the proof.

Proof of Proposition 2. It follows (5) and (14) that

$$X_{It} = (r(t)/r_1)(x - \delta \bar{e}),$$

which proves (11). We now assume that (9) holds and determine that demand X_{Ut}. The uninformed trader's prior distribution of θ is diffuse (uniform over real line) so that, using (9), the posterior distribution of θ is normally distributed with a mean of $P - \bar{e}/(r_1 s + (r - r_1)/(1/s + (1/r_1 s)^2 V)) = w_\lambda$ and a variance of $(1/r_1 s)^2 V$. Therefore,

$$E[u|P] = w_\lambda, \text{ and} \tag{A1}$$

$$\mathrm{Var}[u|P] = 1/s + (1/r_1 s)^2 V. \tag{A2}$$

By substituting into (7), using the expressions for (9), (A1), and (A2), we obtain

$$X_{Ut} = (r(t)\bar{e}/(r_1 s + (r - r_1)/(1/s + (1/r_1 s)^2 V)))/(1/s + (1/r_1 s)^2 V),$$

which simplifies, using (13), to

$$X_{Ut} = (r(t)/(r - r_1))\delta \bar{e},$$

which proves (12).

Consequently, uniformed traders purchase $X_U = \delta \bar{e}$ of the risky asset, whereas the informed traders purchase $X_I = (1 - \delta)\bar{e} + (x - \bar{e})$ of the risky asset. Clearly the equilibrium condition (8) is satisfied, which proves that (9) is an equilibrium price function. Q.E.D.

Proof of Proposition 4. From (9) and (10) we see that $\mathrm{Var}[P] = 1/h + (1/r_1 s)^2 V$ with no public information. With public information $\mathrm{Var}[P] = 1/h + (1/r_1^D s)^2 V$. Now use $r_1^D > r_1$. Q.E.D.

Proof of Lemma 1. Let W be a wealth-random variable with T a scalar transfer payment. The following uses the basic relationship

$$-E(\exp[-(W + T)/r(t)]) = -E(\exp[-W/r(t)])\exp[-T/r(t)].$$

By giving each trader $t f_B(t) - f_A(t)$ as a transfer payment, each trader is indifferent between equilibrium A' (A transformed by the transfer payments) and equilibrium B. By hypothesis this is a negative-sum set of transfer payments. Clearly by going to a zero-sum set of transfer payments we can achieve a Pareto improvement. Furthermore, the very same argument shows that there is no zero-sum set of transfer payments, making a transformed B preferred to A. Q.E.D.

Proof of Proposition 5. Let the expected utility of wealth of trader t conditioned on (θ,x) equal $-\exp[-f_A(t)/r(t)]$ with public information and equal $-\exp[-f_B(t)/r(t)]$ with no public information.

It will clarify the analysis if we rewrite (15), (16), and (17), using (4), as

$$V_{It}(\theta,x) = -\exp[-((\bar{B}(t)+e(t)P)/r(t)+X_{It}(\theta-P)/r(t)-(X_{It}^2/2r(t)^2s))],$$

$$V_{Ut}(\theta,x) = -\exp[-((\bar{B}(t)+e(t)P)/r(t)+X_{Ut}(\theta-P)/r(t)-(X_{Ut}^2/2r(t)^2s))],$$

$$\text{and } V_{Lt}(\theta,x) = -\exp[-(e(t)+(x-\bar{e})/\gamma)P/r(t)].$$

Recalling the definition of $\bar{e}$ and using (8) it follows that the coefficient of P will cancel when we integrate for the obvious reason that the quantity of risky assets demanded equals the quantity supplied. Therefore,

$$\int_0^{1+\gamma} f_B(t)dt = \int_0^1 \bar{B}(t)dt + x\theta + \int_0^\lambda -(X_{It}^2/2r(t)s)dt + \int_\lambda^1 -(X_{Ut}^2/2r(t)s)dt.$$

Similarly, and using (11),

$$\int_0^{1+\gamma} f_A(t)dt = \int_0^1 \bar{B}(t)dt + x\theta + \int_0^1 -([r(t)x/r]^2/2r(t)s)dt.$$

By (11) and (12), we have that

$$\int_0^{1+\gamma} (f_A(t)-f_B(t))dt = -x^2/2rs + (x-\delta\bar{e})^2/2r_1s + (\delta\bar{e})^2/2(r-r_1)s. \quad \text{(A3)}$$

The righthand side of (A3) is a convex function of x and is minimized by $x = r\delta\bar{e}/(r-r_1)$. (For this value of x the public-information and the no-public-information equilibriums are identical). The righthand side of (A3) is zero when $x = r\delta\bar{e}/(r-r_1)$, and otherwise it is strictly positive. Now apply Lemma 1. Q.E.D.

Proof of Lemma 2. Let $f(x) = \ln((c/x^2)+1)x$. By the fundamental theorem of calculus, $f(x_1)-f(x_2) = \int_{x_2}^{x_1} f'(x)dx$. Therefore, it will suffice to show $f'(x) \geq -c/x^2$. We have $f'(x) = \ln((c/x^2)+1) - 2c/(c+x^2)$. If we write c as αx^2, then it remains to show that

$$g(\alpha) = \ln(1+\alpha) - 2\alpha/(1+\alpha) + \alpha \geq 0$$

for all $\alpha > 0$. Clearly $g(0) = 0$, and $g'(\alpha) = 1/(1+\alpha) + 1 - 2/(1+\alpha)^2 > 0$. Q.E.D.

Proof of Theorem 1. Let V_{It}, V_{Ut}, and V_{Lt} respectively be the expected utilities of the informed, uninformed, and liquidity traders with no public information. It follows from (15) and (16), the hypothesis that $e(t)$ (and hence $\bar{e}$) $= 0$, and Lemma 3 that $V_{It} = -\exp[-(\bar{B}/r(t) + .5\ln(V/r_1^2s + 1))]$, and $V_{Ut} = -\exp[\bar{B}/r(t)]$. Integrating $V_{Lt}(\theta,x)$ in (17), first over θ and then over x followed by the application of Lemma 3, yields

$$V_{Lt} = -\exp[-(-.5(\mu_\theta/\gamma r(t))^2/(-2(1/(\gamma r(t)r_1 s) + 1/(2h\gamma^2 r(t)^2)) + 1/V) + .5\ln(-2V(1/\gamma r(t)r_1 s) + 1/(2h\gamma^2 r(t)^2)) + 1))].$$

With public information, the above equations apply with r_1^D replacing r. The expression for V_{Lt} is well defined by our assumption (18) that the expected utility of liquidity traders is greater than minus infinity. Let the expected utility of wealth of trader t be written as $-\exp[-f_A(t)/r(t)]$ with public information and as $-\exp[-f_B(t)/r(t)]$ with no public information. Since $(-.5(\mu_\theta/\gamma r(t))^2/(-2(1/\gamma r(t)r_1 s + 1/2h\gamma^2 r(t)^2) + 1/V)$ is smaller (more negative) than the same expression with r_1^D substituted for r_1, we can write

$$\int_0^{1+\gamma} (f_A(t) - f_B(t))dt > .5\ln(V/(r_1^D)^2 s + 1)r_1^D - .5\ln(V/r_1^2 s + 1)r_1 +$$
$$\int_1^{1+\gamma}[.5\ln(-2V(1/\gamma r(t)r_1^D s) + 1/(2h\gamma^2 r(t)^2)) + 1) - .5\ln(-2V(1/\gamma r(t)r_1 s) + 1/(2h\gamma^2 r(t)^2)) + 1)]r(t)dt.$$

We now use Lemma 2 plus the fact that for $1 > x > y > 0$, $\ln(x) - \ln(y) > x - y$, to conclude that

$$\int_0^{1+\gamma} (f_A(t) - f_B(t))dt > .5V/r_1^D s - .5V/r_1 s - V/r_1^D s + V/r_1 s > 0.$$

Now apply Lemma 1. Q.E.D.

Equations used in calculating Table 1. Let x be normally distributed with a mean of $\bar{e}$ and a variance of V. Then a straightforward calculation shows that for scalars t_1 and $t_2 > -1/2V$,

$$E(\exp[-(t_1 x + t_2 x^2)]) = \frac{1}{\sqrt{2t_2 V + 1}} \exp[-.5((2\bar{e}^2 t_2/V - t_1^2 + 2\bar{e}t_1/V)/(2t_2 + 1/V))].$$

This equation is applied to each of the three categories of traders. For example, for liquidity traders with $\lambda^D = 1.0$,

$$V_{Lt} = -E(\exp[-((x - \bar{e})/\gamma r(t))(\theta - x/rs)])$$
$$= -E(\exp[-(((x - \bar{e})/\gamma r(t))\mu_\theta - .5((x - \bar{e})/\gamma r(t))^2/h + (\bar{e}/\gamma r(t)rs)x - (1/\gamma r(t)rs)x^2)]).$$

By collecting the coefficients of x and x^2 one can apply the above equation.

Proof of Proposition 7. In the first example public information will pass the compensation test. The parameters in this example are $\gamma = 1, e(t) = 0, \bar{B}(t) = 0$, and $r(t) = 1$ for all $0 \leq t \leq 2$. As in the numerical simulations in Section 4, $V = .02$, $s = 250$, $h = 250$, and $\mu_\theta = 1$. The liquidity traders are identical and the nonliquidity traders are identical and each has measure 1.

With public information, the proof of Theorem 1 is applicable and the expected utility of each informed trader is $V_{It}^D = -\exp[-.5\ln(V/r^2 s + 1)] =$

$-\exp[-.5\ln((.02/250)+1)]$, where the superscript D stands for disclosure. The equations used in calculating Table 1 are applicable, and the expected utility for liquidity traders is

$$V_{Lt}^{D} = -E(\exp[-(t_1 x + t_2 x^2)]), \tag{A4}$$

where $t_1 = \mu_\theta/(\gamma r(t)) = 1$ and $t_2 = -.5/((\gamma r(t))^2 h) - 1/(\gamma r(t)rs) = -1.5/250$. Applying Lemma 3 yields

$$V_{Lt}^{D} = -\exp[-(.5\ln((-.06/250)+1)-.5/((-3/250)+50))].$$

Next we consider our example without public information. We substitute $r(t)x/r$ for X_t and (20) for P in (4) and integrate over θ to obtain

$$V_{Ut}(x) = -\exp[-(x^2/2r^2)(1/s + 1/h)].$$

Applying Lemma 3 yields $V_{Ut} = -\exp[-.5\ln((V/r^2)(1/s + 1/h) + 1)] = -\exp[-.5\ln((.04/250)+1)]$. For liquidity traders we use (20) to obtain

$$V_{Lt}(x) = -\exp[-(x/(\gamma r(t)))(\mu_\theta - (x/r)(1/s + 1/h))].$$

Thus V_{Lt} can be expressed in the form (A4) with $t_1 = \mu_\theta/(\gamma r(t)) = 1$ and $t_2 = -(1/(\gamma r(t)r))(1/s + 1/h) = -2/250$. Applying Lemma 3 yields

$$V_{Lt} = -\exp[-(.5\ln((-.08/250)+1)-.5/((-4/250)+50))].$$

Since

$$.5\ln((.02/250)+1)+.5\ln((-.06/250)+1)-.5/((-3/250)+50) >$$
$$.5\ln((.04/250)+1)+.5\ln((-.08/250)+1)-.5/((-4/250)+50),$$

public information passes the compensation test with these parameters using Lemma 1.

Now we keep the same parameters except that $r(t)=2$ for the nonliquidity traders and consequently $r=2$. With public information, $V_{It}^{D} = -\exp[-.5\ln((.02/1000)+1)]$ and

$$V_{Lt}^{D} = -\exp[-(.5\ln((-.04/250)+1)-.5/((-2/250)+50))].$$

Without public information, $V_{Ut} = -\exp[-.5\ln((.04/1,000)+1)]$ and

$$V_{Lt} = -\exp[-(.5\ln((-.04/250)+1)-.5/((-2/250)+50))].$$

With these parameters, no public information is Pareto preferred to public information and *a fortiori* passes the compensation test.

REFERENCES

Allen, F. 1987. "The Social Value of Asymmetric Information." Working Paper. U. of Pennsylvania, Finance Department.

Broadway, R. 1974. "The Welfare Foundations of Cost–Benefit Analysis." *Economic Journal*, 84 (December), 926–939.

Copeland, T., and D. Galai. 1983. "Information Effects on the Bid–Ask Spread." *Journal of Finance* 38 (December), 1457–1469.

Cyert, R., and M. DeGroot. 1987. *Bayesian Analysis and Uncertainty in Economic Theory*. Totowa, N.J.: Rowman & Littlefield.

Diamond, D. 1985. "Optimal Release of Information by Firms." *Journal of Finance* 40 (September), 1071–1094.

Glosten, L., and P. Milgrom. 1985. "Bid, Ask and Transaction Prices in a Specialist Market with Heterogeneously Informed Traders." *Journal of Financial Economics* 14 (March), 71–100.

Grossman, S., and O. Hart. 1981. "The Allocational Role of Takeover Bids in Situations of Asymmetric Information." *Journal of Finance* 36 (May), 252–270.

Grossman, S., and J. Stiglitz. 1980. "On the Impossibility of Informationally Efficient Markets." *American Economic Review* 70 (June), 393–408.

Hakansson, N. 1981. "On the Politics of Accounting Disclosure and Measurement: An Analysis of Economic Incentives." *Journal of Accounting Research* 19 (Supplement), 1–35.

Hakansson, N., J. G. Kunkel, and J. Ohlson. 1982. "Sufficient and Necessary Conditions for Information to Have Social Value in Pure Exchange." *Journal of Finance* 37 (December), 1169–1181.

Harberger, A. 1971. "Three Basic Postulates for Applied Welfare Economics." *Journal of Economic Literature* 9 (September), 785–797.

Hartigan, J. 1964. "Invariant Prior Distributions." *Annals of Mathematical Statistics* 35 (June), 836–845.

Hicks, J. 1941. "The Rehabilitation of Consumers' Surplus." *Review of Economic Studies* 8 (February), 108–116.

Hirshleifer, J. 1971. "The Private and Social Value of Information and the Reward to Inventive Activity." *American Economic Review* 61 (September), 561–574.

Ibbotson, R., and R. Sinquefield. 1982. *Stocks, Bonds, Bills and Inflation: The Past and Future*. Charlottesville: Financial Research Analysts' Foundation.

Indjejikian, R. 1988. "The Impact of Information on the Extent of Agreement among Investors: A New Perspective on Firm Disclosures." Ph.D. diss. U. of Pennsylvania, Managerial Science and Applied Economics.

Judd, K. 1985. "The Law of Large Numbers with a Continuum of IID Random Variables." *Journal of Economic Theory* 35 (February), 19–25.

Laffont, J. 1985. "On the Welfare Analysis of Rational Expectations Equilibria with Asymmetric Information." *Econometrica* 53 (January), 1–29.

Lee, C. J. 1987. "Accounting Infrastructure and Economic Development." *Journal of Accounting and Public Policy* 6 (Summer), 75–85.

Lev, B. 1988. "Toward a Theory of Equitable and Efficient Accounting Policy." *The Accounting Review* 63 (January), 1–22.

Lippman, S., and J. McCall. 1986. "An Operational Measure of Liquidity." *American Economic Review* 76 (March), 43–55.

Little, I. 1957. *A Critique of Welfare Economics*, 2nd ed. London: Oxford University Press.

Mansfield, E. 1985. *Micro-Economics*, 5th ed. New York: W. W. Norton.

Mirrlees, J. 1971. "An Exploration of the Theory of Optimum Income Taxation." *Review of Economic Studies* 38 (April), 175–208.

Ng, Y. 1984. "Quasi-Pareto Social Improvements." *American Economic Review* 74 (December), 1033–1050.

Ohlson, J. 1987. *The Theory of Financial Markets and Information*. Amsterdam: North-Holland.

Ross, S. 1983. "Accounting and Economics." *The Accounting Review* 58 (April), 375–380.

Sen, A. 1970. *Collective Choice and Social Welfare*. San Francisco: Holden-Day.

Small, K. 1987. "A Constitutional Rationale for Welfare Measurement." Working Paper. U. of California at Irvine, Department of Economics (January).

Verrecchia, R. 1982a. "Information Acquisition in a Noisy Rational Expectations Economy." *Econometrica* 50 (November), 1415–1430.

Verrecchia, R. 1982b. "The Use of Mathematical Models in Financial Accounting." *Journal of Accounting Research* 20 (Supplement), 1–55.

Villegas, C. 1977. "Inner Statistical Inference." *Journal of the American Statistical Association* 72 (June), 453–458.

Wilson, R. 1983. "Auditing: Perspectives from Multi-Person Decision Theory." *The Accounting Review* 58 (April), 305–318.

Comments

RICHARD E. KIHLSTROM*

The aim of the paper is to study the welfare effects of public disclosure requirements. For this purpose, the authors use a variant of the rational expectations model introduced in Grossman and Stiglitz (1980). In the model, as in many recent models of this type, there are both liquidity traders and nonliquidity traders. These traders choose portfolios of a risky stock and a riskless bond. The liquidity traders' portfolio behavior is exogenous to the model and, as the authors point out, can be interpreted as being motivated by life-cycle considerations. The nonliquidity traders can choose to be either informed or uninformed and, in making this choice, they compare the cost of being informed to the benefits obtained from the information. Since this is a rational-expectations equilibrium model, the uninformed traders use equilibrium price observations to infer, to the extent possible, the information of the informed traders.

In this setting, the authors interpret public disclosure requirements as leading to reductions in the cost of information, which increases the equilibrium number of informed traders. Thus, the authors study the welfare effects of disclosure requirements by investigating the impact of increases in the equilibrium number of informed traders. Proposition 5 and Theorem 1 give conditions under which welfare is improved, in the sense of the Kaldor–Hicks–Scitovsky compensation test, by public disclosure requirements. In Section 4.2, numerical simulations are used to obtain the same conclusions for three examples in which the restrictive assumptions of Theorem 1 are relaxed. The authors emphasize that, although the behavior of liquidity traders is not modeled, their welfare is considered in the analysis.

Theoretical investigations of this kind inevitably are based on modeling choices and assumptions, and the interest of the results can depend heavily on the acceptability of the choices and the plausibility of the assumptions. Different modeling choices can also lead to very different conclusions. The authors' choice to model disclosure requirements as reductions in the cost of information is clearly plausible and natural, and it is obviously

*The Wharton School, University of Pennsylvania.

interesting to know that welfare is improved by information cost reductions. The interest of this result does not, however, depend crucially on the interpretation of the cost reduction as having arisen because of a disclosure requirement. As the authors point out in Section 6, and as I would like to emphasize, there are equally plausible alternative approaches to the introduction of disclosure requirements. In Diamond (1985), for example, disclosure is interpreted as the release of public information that augments the information of both informed and uninformed traders. The comparative static analysis of the effects of this kind of disclosure is more complicated, and it leads to different results than those obtained when disclosure reduces information costs. In Diamond's analysis, disclosure does not increase the equilibrium number of informed traders; on the contrary, it reduces that number. The reduction in the number of informed traders caused by the disclosure of public information actually improves the welfare of all nonliquidity traders by reducing the amount expended for information and simultaneously reducing the information of the uninformed. The reduction in the equilibrium amount of information received by the uninformed raises the nonliquidity traders' welfare by the mechanism made familiar by Hirshleifer's (1971) analysis. In the Miller–Copeland analysis, the welfare of all nonliquidity traders is reduced because the disclosure increases the equilibrium number of informed traders. Diamond does not consider the welfare of liquidity traders.

A very different alternative approach to the modeling of disclosure is that introduced in Grossman (1981), Grossman and Hart (1980), and Milgrom (1981). Grossman considers the case of a seller who knows the quality of the good he supplies to an uninformed buyer. He demonstrates that, if lying is impossible, the seller will reveal the quality of his product even if there are no disclosure requirements. Thus, disclosure requirements are unnecessary because they have no effect on the amount of information obtained by buyers. Milgrom obtains a similar result. Grossman and Hart apply Grossman's argument to the analysis of disclosure by ''corporate raiders,'' an analysis that is more closely related to the financial market analysis of the Miller–Copeland paper. A substantial literature, including papers by Farrell (1985), Matthews and Postlewaite (1985), and Milgrom and Roberts (1986), has now arisen investigating the robustness of the Grossman, Grossman–Hart, and Milgrom revelation result. An important feature of the models analyzed in all of this literature is that the disclosure is made by an ''interested party.'' In the Miller–

Copeland paper and the Diamond paper, the interests of the firm or firm managers making the disclosure are not considered.

In obtaining proposition 5 and Theorem 1, the authors have assumed that the uninformed traders do not know the "true" *a priori* distribution of the parameter that becomes known to the informed traders. The uninformed traders are, thus, assumed to use a "diffuse" prior in place of the true one. This is an assumption that I find less appealing and the results obtained using it are, I believe, less interesting than Theorem 7, which assumes that the true prior is known to the uninformed traders. Allen (1987) has also obtained a welfare result very similar to Theorem 7. Allen's result is stated as proposition 6 in the paper.

Miller and Copeland choose not to analyze the influence of disclosure on production and investment decisions. This choice is explained by the authors' expectation that such an analysis is likely to yield ambiguous results. This expectation is based on the well-known fact that the welfare results of Hirshleifer and others demonstrating that information can reduce welfare do not necessarily extend to the case of production economies. The ambiguity in the welfare effects of information is introduced because information helps improve the allocation of resources to production. I agree with the authors' view that an analysis without production is important and interesting in itself. However, the impact of information on production decisions is important and should also be analyzed. Indeed, I regard the Miller–Copeland analysis as an important first step toward a more complete analysis in which production is also considered. In contrast to expectations, the Miller–Copeland results suggest that when production is introduced, welfare will be unambiguously improved by more information. The welfare gains shown to exist by the authors should be augmented by the gains obtained because information improves the allocation of productive resources.

REFERENCES

Allen, F. 1987. "The Social Value of Asymmetric Information." Unpublished working paper, University of Pennsylvania.
Diamond, D. 1985. "Optimal Release of Information by Firms." *Journal of Finance* 40 (September), 1071–1094.
Farrell, J. 1985. "Voluntary Disclosure: Robustness of the Unraveling Result and Comments on Its Importance." In R. Grieson (Ed.), *Proceedings of the U. C. Conference on Antitrust and Regulation.* Lexington Books, 91–103.
Grossman, S. 1981. "The Informational Role of Warranties and Private Disclosure about Product Quality." *Journal of Law and Economics* 24, 461–484.

Grossman, S., and O. Hart. 1980. "Disclosure Laws and Takeover Bids." *Journal of Finance* 40, 323–334.

Grossman, S., and J. Stiglitz. 1980. "On the Impossibility of Informationally Efficient Markets." *American Economic Review* 70 (June), 393–408.

Hirshleifer, J. 1971. "The Private and Social Value of Information and the Reward to Inventive Activity." *American Economic Review* 61 (September), 561–574.

Matthews, S., and A. Postlewaite. 1985. "Quality Testing and Disclosure." *Rand Journal of Economics* 16, 328–340.

Milgrom, P. 1981. "Good News and Bad News." *Bell Journal of Economics* 12, 380–391.

Milgrom, P., and J. Roberts. 1986. "Relying on the Information of Interested Parties." *Rand Journal of Economics* 17, 18–32.

The Globalization of Information and Capital Mobility

WILLIAM H. BRANSON* AND DWIGHT M. JAFFEE**

The trend toward globalization of information in financial markets has appeared to accelerate in recent years. Perhaps most importantly, the plans for ''Europe 1992'' provide for better flows of information in both goods and securities markets for the major European economies. The planned changes, for example, should lead to more uniform reporting and accounting systems. The effects of such improvements in the flow of information in financial markets are generally considered to be beneficial, since they create more integrated capital markets and more mobile capital flows. Given the amount of attention that is being paid to ''Europe 1992,'' it would seem timely to develop a more detailed evaluation of the likely effects of improved information.

It is disappointing, therefore, to find that portfolio selection theory has not focused on analyzing the effects of an improvement in the quality of information, such as might arise from the forthcoming European changes. Indeed, Robert Merton's presidential address for the American Finance Association (Merton, 1987) was directed at precisely this issue. Of course, there is an extensive literature that studies the role of such factors as transactions costs, taxes, and capital controls on international capital mobility.[1] However, as we discuss later, the effects of imperfect capital markets may differ substantially from the effects of imperfect information.

The main objective for this paper is to provide a framework for analyzing the effects of the globalization of information. We focus, in particular, on how the globalization of information influences real interest rate spreads—differences in the levels of real interest rates among countries. We start, in Section 1, by introducing the factors that lead to real interest rate spreads. Section 2 then looks at the sources of imperfect information and at how the quality of information may vary among inves-

*Woodrow Wilson School, Princeton University and NBER.
**Woodrow Wilson School, Princeton University.
1. For recent studies, see Adler and Dumas (1983), Obstfeld (1986), and Frankel (1989).

tors. Section 3 provides a formal portfolio selection model that links real interest rate spreads with imperfect information. Section 4 develops the main conclusions concerning the effects of the globalization of information.

1. REAL INTEREST RATE SPREADS

Frankel and MacArthur (1988) provide a useful framework for analyzing the factors that cause real interest rates to vary across countries. The real interest rate spread is defined as:

(1)
$$r - r^* = (i - \pi_p) - (i^* - \pi_p^*)$$
$$= (i - i^*) - (\pi_p - \pi_p^*)$$

where r is the real interest rate, i is the nominal interest rate, π_p is the expected inflation rate, and asterisks represent foreign variables. By adding and subtracting the expected depreciation of the home currency π_e and then doing the same with the forward discount δ, equation (1) becomes:

(2)
$$r - r^* = (i - i^* - \pi_e) + (\pi_e - \pi_p + \pi_p^*)$$

and

(3)
$$r - r^* = (i - i^* - \delta) + (\delta - \pi_e) + (\pi_e - \pi_p + \pi_p^*).$$

Equation (2) shows that the real interest rate spread can be expressed as two terms—first the *uncovered* interest rate spread $(i - i^* - \pi_e)$ and second the expected real exchange rate depreciation $(\pi_e - \pi_p + \pi_p^*)$. This means that real interest rate spreads can result from factors in either financial markets—the failure of uncovered interest rate parity (UIP)— or real markets—the failure of purchasing power parity (PPP).

Since the expected change in the exchange rate, π_e, is not observable, it is difficult to evaluate empirically whether deviations from UIP or PPP are the more important source of real interest rate spreads. Based on their empirical evidence, Frankel and MacArthur conclude that expected real exchange rate depreciation is the more influential of these two sources of real interest rate spreads. The evidence of Adler and Lehmann (1983), however, implies that PPP may still hold on an *ex ante*, if not *ex post*, basis. In this case, deviations from UIP would have to be the primary source of real interest rate spreads.

In interpreting equation (2), it is also important to recognize that the

UIP and PPP terms may not be independent. That is, deviations from UIP may create deviations from PPP, and vice versa. In particular, the model in Section 3 below illustrates a case in which larger PPP deviations are the source of larger UIP deviations.

Equation (3) shows that the uncovered interest rate spread can be further decomposed into two terms, the first containing the *covered* interest rate spread $(i - i^* - \delta)$ and the second containing the forward exchange market risk premium $(\delta - \pi_e)$. This means that uncovered interest rate parity can fail to hold either because covered interest rate parity fails to hold or because there is a forward exchange market risk premium. The standard view in the recent literature, consistent with the evidence of Frankel and MacArthur, is that the *covered* interest rate differential is likely to be small empirically.[2] This implies that an exchange market risk premium is the most likely financial market source of real interest rate spreads.

Given that *covered* interest rate parity does hold, it is logically equivalent to represent the exchange market risk premium either as a deviation from *uncovered* interest parity (as in equation (2)) or as the difference between the expected exchange rate depreciation and the forward discount (as in equation (3)). Whichever interpretation is preferred, the international portfolio choice literature indicates that a variety of specific conditions in the two countries, such as unequal supplies of wealth and securities, or unequal commodity (consumption) preferences, can be the source of the risk premiums (see Adler and Dumas, 1983). The model developed in Section 3 illustrates how this works.

Information plays a number of important roles in determining exchange market risk premiums. First, uncertainty is a necessary condition for risk premiums to exist at all. Otherwise, if investment outcomes were known with certainty, then risk-free arbitrage would eliminate all risk premiums. Second, the particular form taken by stochastic processes can affect the measure used for uncovered interest rate parity. For example, for the model developed in Section 3 with continuous-time stochastic processes, the *parity* relationship between interest rates includes covariance terms that are omitted from equation (2). Third, if the amount of uncertainty increases, then the size of risk premiums will generally rise. This result is illustrated in Section 3. Fourth, asymmetrical access to information—

2. Frankel and MacArthur (1988) refer to potential deviations from *covered* interest rate parity as *country* risk, since such deviations would arise from capital controls and other country-specific restrictions on capital flows.

meaning that investors face different levels of uncertainty—can affect both the size and the specific form of risk premiums.

Even though information affects exchange market risk premiums in these various ways, the effects of changing the amount of information have not been closely studied. In this paper, we start to redress this shortcoming of the literature by analyzing the role of imperfect information as a source of risk premiums and real interest rate spreads.

Real Rate Spreads for Risky Securities

Real interest rate spread equations, such as equations (1), (2), and (3), have been analyzed traditionally only for securities that have no default risk. To consider imperfect information, however, it is essential to include securities with default risk. Otherwise, if the securities are assumed to be free of default risk, then investors have no need to obtain information and there is thus no role for imperfect information. The solution is to expand equation (3) to cover *risky* securities—which can be interpreted as either equity securities or risky debt securities.

For this purpose, let us suppose that r and r^* are the expected real returns and i and i^* are the expected nominal returns on two *risky* bonds. The expected returns (both nominal and real) on the two securities may include *risk premiums* that compensate investors for bearing the risk. Such risk premiums will tend to be greater the more risk-averse are investors and the greater the extent to which the risk of default is not diversifiable—as, for example, when default depends on the macroeconomic performance of the economy.

If we denote the risk premiums on the home and foreign securities as τ and τ^* respectively, then equation (2) can be modified by adding and subtracting τ and τ^*:

(4) $\qquad r - r^* = [(i - \tau) - (i^* - \tau^*) - \pi_e] + (\tau - \tau^*) + (\pi_e - \pi_p + \pi_p^*).$

The terms $(i - \tau)$ and $(i^* - \tau^*)$ are the expected returns *net of risk premiums* for the home and foreign securities respectively, whereas the term $(\tau - \tau^*)$ is the difference between the two risk premiums. Of course, if the two securities have equal levels of risk and investors evaluate the risk without regard to the country or currency in which the securities are issued, then τ might equal τ^*. But even with equal risk, unequal risk premiums may still arise whenever the demand/supply balance for risk is different in the two countries. In Section 3, we analyze how the relationship between real interest rate spreads and security risk is affected by improved flows of information.

2. THE "GLOBALIZATION" OF INFORMATION

We next consider how differences in information affect international portfolio decisions and the level of risk premiums. The available information concerning a country's securities may vary depending on such factors as the size or stage of development of the country or the location of the investors. As one case, information may be of lower quality in smaller or in less-developed countries, reflecting the absence of economies of scale for creating uniform accounting standards or for carrying out investments that provide additional information.

As another case, the quality of security information in each country may be higher for local investors than for foreign investors. That is, local investors generally will have an advantage in locating and interpreting information about local securities. In this context, "Europe 1992" provides an example where the quality of information for the securities of a region is about to improve. As these countries adopt more uniform accounting and reporting standards, the informational advantages of local European investors relative to foreign investors might disappear.

To evaluate the effects of an improvement in information, we have to quantify what we mean by the *quality* of information. We do that here within the context of mean/variance portfolio selection models. In these models, investors require parameter values for the expected return vector and the variance/covariance matrix of returns. Standard treatments of portfolio selection theory assume either that investors know these parameters *with certainty* or that *estimates of the parameters* can be used as if they were certain, given that the true values are unknown. In either case, this leaves no room for situations in which there exists a range of quality levels for information. An alternative framework is thus necessary in order to analyze the effects of changing the quality of information.

Parameter Uncertainty and Estimation Risk

A more general, and for us more useful, approach for dealing with information can be derived from the finance literature concerned with *parameter uncertainty*.[3] The starting point is to recognize that because

3. See, for example, Barry and Brown (1985), Bawa, Brown, and Klein (1979), or Brown (1979).

investors generally do not know the true parameters, they have to use statistical techniques to construct estimates. Moreover, although the estimation process provides a set of *point estimates* for the parameters, a band of *uncertainty* necessarily remains. The parameter uncertainty literature analyzes how this estimation risk is properly incorporated in portfolio selection decisions and models.

To illustrate how this works, assume that the true information is given by the set $\theta = \{\mu, \Sigma\}$, with μ the expected return vector and Σ the variance/covariance matrix. The investor maintains a *diffuse* (uninformative) prior concerning the parameters, but has access to T data observations from which the parameters can be estimated. Let the resulting point estimates for the parameters be $\theta^* = \{\mu^*, \Sigma^*\}$. Although this example uses the number of observations T to measure the quality of information, the parameter uncertainty literature recognizes that other improvements in information quality can affect the variance/covariance matrix in a comparable manner.[4]

Whereas standard portfolio selection theory treats the point estimates θ^* as if they were the true parameters, the parameter uncertainty literature uses the *predictive distribution* to take parameter uncertainty into account (see Bawa, Brown, and Klein, 1979). The upshot is that different parameter values, namely $\theta = \{\mu^*, (1+[1/T])\Sigma^*\}$, are used for making portfolio decisions. In particular, the estimated variance/covariance matrix Σ^* is multiplied by an adjustment factor, $1+(1/T)$, which is greater than 1.

The adjustment factor approaches 1 only as the number of observations T approaches infinity—that is, as the information becomes certain. Otherwise, the effect of parameter uncertainty is to raise the size of the perceived variance/covariance matrix. We use this approach to model an improvement in information as if it created a reduction in the parameters of the variance/covariance matrix used by investors for determining their optimal portfolios.

An alternative approach is illustrated in the paper by Michael Adler and Bhaskar Prasad, "Optimal Foreign Currency Hedging When Information Is Imperfect," which also appears in this symposium. In their approach, new information becomes steadily available to the investor, who uses it to update the prior density. In our approach, in contrast, the change in the quality of information is a one-time event.

---

4. See, in particular, Barry and Brown (1985), p. 413.

Capital Market Imperfections and Informational Imperfections

The *parameter uncertainty* model for imperfect information can be compared with the *barriers to international investment* model for imperfect capital markets.[5] In the barriers model, capital market imperfections—such as transactions costs and comparable impediments to trade—are treated as implicit taxes on the returns to foreign investment. Reducing these barriers to international investment thus raises the level of the expected return for investors. In contrast, with the parameter uncertainty model, improving information quality decreases the size of the perceived variance/covariance parameters.

The main point here is that an improvement in information quality, such as the plans for "Europe 1992," can affect investor decisions through the variance/covariance matrix without directly affecting the expected returns. Since an increase in expected returns may seem more tangible than a reduction in parameter uncertainty, an informational change may appear less important, even when it creates exactly the same increase in investor welfare.

Endogenous Information Quality

Our discussion has so far treated information quality as an exogenous factor in the model, which is sensible when looking at the effects of developments such as "Europe 1992." There are other contexts, however, in which the quality of information should be treated as an endogenous variable.

One important case occurs when access to information requires an expenditure of resources by the investor.[6] The cost of information can be either a fixed cost or a variable cost that rises with the amount of information. The cost of information may also differ between local and foreign investors, with local investors facing lower costs than foreign investors for obtaining local security information.

Even when local investors have lower information costs, their expected returns after subtracting information costs may also be lower, since the lower cost of information will cause them to purchase more information.

---

5. See Black (1974), Stulz (1981), and the survey in Adler and Dumas (1983).
6. See Ho and Michaely (1988) for a recent model of this type.

Of course, local investors will also be receiving the benefits of higher-quality information. The upshot is that information may affect both the expected return vector and the variance/covariance matrix in equilibrium, thus combining what we earlier called the barriers and the parameter uncertainty models.

Another case of endogenous information arises when investors can infer information by observing the market price. In this case, the market will include both *informed* investors who can directly obtain information at a low cost and *uninformed* investors for whom the cost of information is high, even prohibitive. Although the uninformed investors are at a disadvantage, Grossman and Stiglitz (1980) have shown that the market price may provide uninformed investors with free access to the information held by the informed investors. To the extent that this happens, it reduces the incentive for informed investors to allocate resources to obtain information. Thus, even when information is endogenous, it is still likely to be imperfect.

Another aspect of markets with informed and uninformed investors is that the welfare effects of improved information become more complex. For example, Stein's (1987) model develops a case in which the entry of additional uninformed traders creates random variations in market prices, which decrease the welfare of the informed traders. In the context of "Europe 1992," a comparable result would be that improving the quality of information available to non-European investors could reduce the welfare of European investors, who lose some of their advantage in terms of information.

Still another effect of endogenous information—*adverse selection*—may arise when particular classes of investors can be explicitly recognized. A good example in the case of international investment is that local borrowers (and other sellers of securities) may realize that less information is available to foreign investors than to local investors. As a result, local borrowers may offer foreign investors securities that have an inferior expected return/risk ratio compared to the securities offered to local investors. Foreign investors will then tend to withdraw from such markets, in the same way that they do when facing investment barriers or lower information quality.

The importance of adverse selection will vary across markets, depending on the extent to which the identity of local and foreign (or informed and uninformed) investors is relevant. For example, adverse selection should not be a serious problem on organized stock markets, where the identity of the traders does not directly enter into the transaction.[7] On the other hand, in banking markets, the quality of loans made critically depends on the information available to the lender. In this case, foreign banks may find that their borrower applicant pool is of lower quality than the pool available to local banks.

Conclusions regarding Information

The portfolio selection model that we develop in the next section provides a convenient but simplified starting point for evaluating the effects of higher-quality information. The model is based on the parameter uncertainty approach, in that higher-quality information is assumed to reduce the size of the variance/covariance parameters, which are treated as exogenous. We also consider various cases in which domestic and foreign investors have differential access to information. Since the supply of information is exogenous, however, there is no explicit role for adverse selection.

3. A MODEL OF THE EQUILIBRIUM RISK PREMIUM

This section of the paper develops a formal model of the equilibrium risk premium on nominal risky assets and shows how it is affected by improvements in information—interpreted as reductions, in several ways, of the estimated variance of returns. The model has two risky assets—one domestic and one foreign—and two representative investors—domestic and foreign—who hold portfolios composed of both assets. The returns on both assets follow stochastic processes in continuous time, as do the exchange rate and the two price levels used to deflate wealth by the two investors.[8] This represents an extension of the models developed in Branson and Henderson (1985) and Fraga (1986).

We first derive the individual investors' portfolio demands, following the example in Branson and Henderson. We then solve for the market equilibrium risk premium, following the example in Fraga. The terms in

7. If necessary, foreign traders could even use local agents to complete their transactions. Of course, *corrupt* local agents can still take advantage of traders, as we have seen recently in some U.S. futures markets.

8. Compared to Branson and Henderson (1985) and Fraga (1986), this sets $\alpha^* = 0$, and makes the returns stochastic, to give us the case of risky assets.

this risk premium can be interpreted as stochastic deviations from uncovered interest parity (UIP) and purchasing power parity (PPP). This analysis unifies the literature on international risk premia, exemplified by Frankel and MacArthur (1988), and the finance literature on portfolio demands.

In the following analysis we study the effects on asset demands and the risk premium of changes in information characterized by estimates of the variance of the stochastic returns. We first look at an improvement in information about the "foreign" asset that is shared by all market participants. Then we study the asymmetric case in which the home investors' estimate of the variance on the foreign asset falls relative to the foreign investors' estimate. This could be interpreted as the effect of an action that reduces the foreign investors' information advantage. We find that in both cases an improvement in information on the foreign asset shifts demand in that direction, reducing the size of the foreign asset's risk premium.

International Asset Demands: Home Investor

We begin with the problem facing the domestic investor, whose real wealth is given by

$$\tilde{W} = \frac{W}{P} = \frac{B + EF}{P},$$

(5)

where B and F are the holdings of domestic and foreign risky assets, E is the nominal exchange rate in units of home currency per unit of foreign exchange, and P is the home price level. There is no riskless asset in the model.

The problem is to choose portfolio shares given by

(6) $B = \lambda W,$

and

(7) $EF = (1 - \lambda)\, W,$

to maximize an objective function given by

(8) $V = \epsilon \left(\frac{d\tilde{W}}{\tilde{W}} \right) - \frac{1}{2} R \, \text{var} \left(\frac{d\tilde{W}}{\tilde{W}} \right),$

where ϵ denotes expected return and var is variance. As discussed in Branson and Henderson (1985), this time-separable form of the objective function, and its mean-variance form, are consistent with a HARA utility function of the form $U = \dfrac{1}{\gamma} C^{\gamma}$, where the coefficient of relative risk aversion in the objective function is $R = \gamma - 1$. The stochastic processes for the rate of return are specified as:

$$\text{(9)} \qquad \frac{dB}{B} = i_b \, dt + \sigma_b \, dz_b$$

and

$$\text{(10)} \qquad \frac{dF}{F} = i_f \, dt + \sigma_f \, dz_f.$$

The exchange rate and two price levels follow stochastic processes given by

$$\text{(11)} \qquad \frac{dE}{E} = \pi_e \, dt + \sigma_e \, dz_e,$$

$$\text{(12)} \qquad \frac{dP}{P} = \pi_p \, dt + \sigma_p \, dz_p,$$

and

$$\text{(13)} \qquad \frac{dP^*}{P^*} = \pi_p^* \, dt + \sigma_p^* \, dz_p^*.$$

Here the returns, the exchange rate, and the price levels all follow geometric Brownian motion with expected drift given by the term in dt and variances σ_i^2. Only P is relevant for the home investor.

To solve the home investor's problem, first take the Ito differential of (5) for $d\tilde{W}$, divide through by expressions (6) and (7) for W/P, and then substitute (9) to (13) into the result.[9] This yields for $d\tilde{W}/\tilde{W}$

9. See Branson and Henderson (1985) for an example of the arithmetic involved.

$$\frac{d\tilde{W}}{\tilde{W}} = [\lambda i_b + (1-\lambda)\ i_f + (1-\lambda)\pi_e - \pi_p + (1-\lambda)\rho_{ef}$$

(14)
$$-\lambda\rho_{bp} - (1-\lambda)\rho_{fp} - (1-\lambda)\rho_{ep} + \sigma_p^2]dt$$

$$+\lambda\sigma_b dz_b + (1-\lambda)\sigma_f dz_f + (1-\lambda)\sigma_e dz_e - \sigma_p dz_p,$$

where the term in dt is the expected return in the objective function in equation (8) and the square of the terms in dz_i is the variance:

$$\text{var}\left[\frac{d\tilde{W}}{\tilde{W}}\right] = \lambda^2\sigma_b^2 + (1-\lambda)^2\sigma_f^2 + (1-\lambda)^2\sigma_e^2 + \sigma_p^2$$

(15)
$$+2[\lambda(1-\lambda)\ (\rho_{bf} + \rho_{be}) + (1-\lambda)\rho_{fe}^2$$

$$-\lambda\rho_{pb} - (1-\lambda)\rho_{pf} - (1-\lambda)\rho_{pe}].$$

In equations (14) and (15) the ρ terms are the covariances, $\rho_{ij} = \sigma_i\ \sigma_j\ r_{ij}$, where r is the correlation coefficient.

Substituting the dt term in (14) into the objective function in (8) for $\epsilon(d\tilde{W}/\tilde{W})$ and the expression in (15) for $\text{var}(d\tilde{W}/\tilde{W})$, differentiating with respect to λ, and solving the first order conditions yield the portfolio demand

(16)
$$\lambda = \frac{D+C+RZ}{RA} = \frac{Z}{A} + \frac{D+C}{RA} = \frac{R-1}{R}\frac{Z}{A} + \frac{1}{R}\frac{D+C+Z}{A},$$

where the terms are:

D = uncovered interest differential = $i_b - i_f - \pi_e$;

C = covariance terms that enter expected return
$$= -\rho_{ef} - (\rho_{bp} - \rho_{fp} - \rho_{ep});$$

A = $\sigma_e^2 + \sigma_f^2 + \sigma_b^2 + 2(\rho_{ef} - \rho_{bf} - \rho_{be}) = \text{var}(B - EF) > 0$;

Z = $\sigma_e^2 + \sigma_f^2 + 2\rho_{ef} - (\rho_{bf} + \rho_{be}) + (\rho_{bp} - \rho_{fp} - \rho_{ep})$.

The demand for the home asset in (16) is written in two separable forms to highlight the role of the minimum-variance portfolio given by $\lambda_{min} = Z/A$.[10] The entire home investor's portfolio in the first separable form can be written as

$$\lambda = \lambda_{min} + \frac{D+C}{RA};$$

---

10. This is the solution for λ obtained by minimizing the portfolio variance in equation (15). See also Branson and Henderson (1985).

(17)
$$1 - \lambda = (1 - \lambda_{min}) - \frac{D + C}{RA}.$$

Here all of wealth is held in the minimum-variance portfolio (i.e., $\lambda_{min} + (1 - \lambda_{min}) = 1$) combined with holdings of a zero net worth speculative portfolio that are inversely proportional to RA. The second separable form of the portfolio in (16) shows it as a weighted average of the minimum-variance portfolio and the portfolio of a ''logarithmic'' investor with $R = 1$ (i.e., $[D + C + Z]/A$). This is the form favored by Adler and Dumas (1983).

We can immediately check the derivative of λ with respect to σ_f^2, which enters A and Z linearly, and D and C not at all. The result is given by

(18)
$$\frac{\partial \lambda}{\partial \sigma_f^2} = \frac{1}{A} (1 - \lambda),$$

which is positive if $\lambda < 1$; that is, if less than all of wealth is held in the home asset. In this case an increase in the home investor's estimate of σ_f^2, holding all covariances constant, increases the share of the home asset in the portfolio (i.e., drives the home investor home). If $\lambda > 1$, so $(1 - \lambda) < 0$, the home investor is borrowing abroad to hold more than all of his wealth in home assets. In this case, $\partial \lambda / \partial \sigma_f^2$ is negative. An increase in σ_f^2 reduces the extent to which the investor borrows abroad.

It will be useful in interpreting later results to study at this point the derivative of λ with respect to σ_f, holding all correlation coefficient r's constant. Using the definition of the covariance in terms of the correlation coefficient $\rho_{fi} = \sigma_i \sigma_f r_{fi}$, we obtain the derivatives of A, C, and Z with respect to σ_f shown later in equations (33). Using those, we obtain the result

(19)
$$\frac{\partial \lambda}{\partial \sigma_f} = \frac{1}{A} \left\{ 2(1 - \lambda)\sigma_f + (2\lambda - 1)\sigma_b \, r_{bf} \right.$$
$$\left. + \left[2(1 - \lambda) - \frac{1}{R} \right] \sigma_e \, r_{ef} - \left(1 - \frac{1}{R} \right) \sigma_p \, r_{pf} \right\}.$$

First we note that if all r's $= 0$, the expression in (19) is equivalent to (18): An increase in σ_f directly increases λ. The sign of the coefficient of $\sigma_b \, r_{bf}$ is unclear. Below we assume that $r_{bf} \approx 0$. The sign of the coefficient of $\sigma_p \, r_{pf}$ is negative; below we assume $r_{pf} \approx 0$. The sign of the coefficient of $\sigma_e \, r_{ef}$ is also unclear. Below we assume $r_{ef} > 0$, so this coefficient should be positive to contribute to an increase in λ. It is sufficient for this coefficient to be positive that $\lambda < 0.5$ assuming $R \geq 1$.

Demand by the Foreign Investor

The foreign investor's real wealth is given by

$$(20) \qquad \tilde{W}^* = \frac{W^*}{P^*} = \frac{(B^*/E) + F^*}{P^*}.$$

The foreign objective function is the same as (8) with $\tilde{W}^*$ substituted for $\tilde{W}$. The foreign investor's portfolio shares are given by

$$(21) \qquad\qquad B^*/E = \lambda^* \, W^*$$

and

$$(22) \qquad\qquad F^* = (1 - \lambda^*) \, W^*.$$

We assume at this stage that the information sets of the two investors are identical, so the foreign investor observes the same stochastic processes (9)–(13) as the home investor. We also assume equal degrees of risk aversion. Then, following the same procedure for solving the foreign investor's portfolio problem as for the home investor yields the foreign demand for the home asset:

$$(23) \qquad \lambda^* = \frac{D + C^* + RZ^*}{RA} = \frac{Z^*}{A} + \frac{D + C^*}{RA}.$$

Here the terms are as already defined for D and A, plus

$$C^* = \sigma_e^2 - \rho_{eb} - (\rho_{bp^*} - \rho_{fp^*} - \rho_{ep^*}), \text{ and}$$

$$Z^* = \sigma_f^2 - (\rho_{bf} - \rho_{ef}) + (\rho_{bp^*} - \rho_{fp^*} - \rho_{ep^*}).$$

Again, the foreign investor's portfolio can be characterized in terms of a minimum-variance portfolio $\lambda^*_{min} = Z^*/A$ and $1 - \lambda^*_{min}$, plus a speculative portfolio inversely proportional to RA.

Again, we can check the effect of an increase in σ_f^2 on the foreign investor's portfolio. Noting that σ_f^2 enters linearly in A and Z^*, and not at all in D or C^*, we have

(24) $$\frac{\partial \lambda^*}{\partial \sigma_f^2} = \frac{1}{A}(1 - \lambda^*) > 0 \text{ if } \lambda^* < 1,$$

similar to the result for the home investor. An increase in the commonly perceived riskiness of the foreign asset, represented by an increase in σ_f^2 holding all ρ's constant, drives both investors toward the home asset.

It will also be useful in interpreting later results to obtain here the derivatives of λ^* with respect to σ_f and σ_b, holding all r's constant. The first will be useful in examining the effect of an increase in identical marketwide information on returns on one asset (here, F) on the equilibrium risk premium D. The second will be useful in looking at the effects of an improvement in each set of investor's information about the returns on the other's assets.

Following the same procedure used earlier for $\partial \lambda / \partial \sigma_f$, we obtain

(25) $$\frac{\partial \lambda^*}{\partial \sigma_f} = \frac{1}{A}\{2(1 - \lambda^*)\,\sigma_f + (2\lambda^* - 1)\,\sigma_b\,r_{bf}$$
$$+ (1 - 2\lambda^*)\,\sigma_e r_{ef} - [(R - 1)/R]\,\sigma_p^*\,r_{p*f}\}.$$

The first two terms are the same as in $\partial \lambda / \partial \sigma_f$, with λ^* in for λ. The sign of the coefficient of the $\sigma_e\,r_{ef}$ term is again unclear, because of conflicting effects from Z^* and A. The sign of the coefficient of the $\sigma_p^*\,r_{p*f}$ is negative. An increase in the covariance of P^* and the return on F make the foreign asset less risky to the foreign investor.

For the effect of σ_b on λ^*, we obtain

(26) $$\frac{\partial \lambda^*}{\partial \sigma_b} = \frac{1}{A}\left[-2\lambda^*\,\sigma_b + (2\lambda^* - 1)\sigma_f\,r_{bf} \right.$$
$$\left. + \left(2\lambda^* - \frac{1}{R}\right)\sigma_e\,r_{eb} + \left(1 - \frac{1}{R}\right)\sigma_p^*\,r_{bp*}\right].$$

In general, we would expect an increase in σ_b to reduce foreign demand for the home bond. The first term in (26) is negative. The sign of the coefficient of $\sigma_f\,r_{bf}$ is unclear, but later we asume $r_{bf} \approx 0$. The coefficient of $\sigma_e\,r_{eb}$ is unclear. We assume $r_{eb} < 0$, so $\lambda^* > 0.5$ would ensure that the term is positive. The coefficient of $\sigma_p^*\,r_{bp*}$ is positive, but we assume $r_{bp*} \approx 0$.

Conditions for Home Asset Preference (HAP)

Since the home and foreign investors deflate nominal wealth by different deflators, we wish to see the conditions under which HAP holds. We define HAP as $\lambda - \lambda^* > 0$. From (16) and (23),

$$\lambda - \lambda^* = \frac{1}{RA}\ [C - C^* + R(Z - Z^*)].$$

Checking the definitions of C, C^*, Z, and Z^* will confirm that $C - C^* = -(Z - Z^*)$, so we have for HAP

(27) $\lambda - \lambda^* = \dfrac{R-1}{RA}(Z - Z^*),$

where:

(28) $$(Z - Z^*) = (\sigma_e^2 - \rho_{be} + \rho_{ef}) - (\rho_{ep} + \rho_{fp} - \rho_{bp})$$
$$+ (\rho_{ep*} + \rho_{fp*} - \rho_{bp*}).$$

If $R > 1$, $(Z - Z^*) > 0$ is sufficient for HAP. How do we interpret this condition?

First, if the assets were not risky, with nonstochastic returns we would have

$$Z - Z^* = \sigma_e^2 + \rho_{ep*} - \rho_{ep},$$

as in Fraga (1986). If PPP were to hold *ex post*, this would be zero.[11] If PPP does not hold *ex post*, as the evidence overwhelmingly indicates (see Frenkel, 1981; or Frankel and MacArthur, 1988), then a larger, more positive ρ_{ep} or a smaller, more negative ρ_{ep*} would *reduce* HAP. This is an intuitive result. From equation (5) for the home investor's real wealth, a larger ρ_{ep} reduces the risk in holding the foreign asset F, reducing λ. From equation (20) for the foreign investor's real wealth, a more negative ρ_{ep*} would reduce the risk in holding the home asset R, increasing λ^*.

Second, if the asset returns are risky but the price indexes are nonstochastic, we have

$$Z - Z^* = \sigma_e^2 - \rho_{be} + \rho_{ef}.$$

If UIP were to hold *ex post*, this would be zero.[12] This, too, is an intuitive result. From the point of view of the home investor, an increase in the

---

11. See Appendix, section 1.
12. See Appendix, section 2.

stochastic deviations from UIP makes the return on the foreign asset F more volatile, increasing λ. From the point of view of the foreign investor, an increase in these deviations makes the return on the home asset more volatile, reducing λ^*.

The remaining terms in $Z - Z^*$ are the covariances of the asset returns and price levels:

$$(\rho_{bp} - \rho_{fp}) + (\rho_{fp^*} - \rho_{bp^*}).$$

From (6) for the home investor's wealth, it is clear that an increase in the covariance of the domestic price level and the home bond return relative to the covariance of the domestic price level and the foreign asset will increase λ. For the foreign investor, an increase in the covariance of F and P^* relative to that of B and P^* will reduce λ^*.

Thus the conditions for HAP are readily interpreted in terms of stochastic deviations from PPP and UIP, and the covariances of nominal asset returns and price levels.

Market Equilibrium with Identical Information

We can now proceed to the solution for the equilibrium risk premium, which we have defined above as $D = i_b - i_f - \pi_e$. Following the way Fraga (1986) set up the problem, we note that market equilibrium for the domestic asset B requires that

(29) $$b = w\lambda + (1 - w)\lambda^*,$$

where $b = B/(W + EW^*)$ and $w = W/(W + EW^*)$. Substitution from equations (16) for λ and (23) for λ^* and solving for D will yield the equilibrium risk premium with identical information and risk aversion:

(30) $$D = RAb - w(R - 1)(Z - Z^*) - (C^* + RZ^*).$$

Here, consistent with the macroeconomic literature, an increase in the relative supply of the domestic asset b will increase the risk premium, and a transfer of wealth to domestic investors will reduce it, assuming HAP holds (i.e., $Z - Z^* > 0$).

One immediate result can be obtained by inspection of the expression for D in (30). The variance and covariance terms all enter linearly in A, Z, Z^*, and C^*. So a proportional increase in all variances, representing a general increase in riskiness, would expand D around zero, making it larger in absolute value by the percentage increase in riskiness, measured by the variances and covariances.

We can now ask what effect a change in the commonly perceived riskiness of the foreign asset has on the equilibrium risk premium D. We have two alternative ways of characterizing this perceived increase in riskiness. The first is an increase in σ_f^2, holding all covariance ρ_{fi} terms constant.[13] This yields a clearcut result. The second is an increase in σ_f, holding all correlation coefficients r_{fi} constant, so that all the ρ_{fi} change by $\sigma_i \, r_{fi} \, d\sigma_f$. These results require further interpretation.

First, we note that σ_f^2 enters only A, Z, and Z^* in equation (30), with each having a partial derivative with respect to σ_f^2 of unity. So on the first interpretation of an increase in the riskiness of F, we have

$$(31) \qquad \frac{\partial D}{\partial \sigma_f^2} = R(b-1) < 0.$$

An increase in the commonly perceived riskiness of F reduces the size of the risk premium on the home asset B. Conversely, if the perceived riskiness of European assets were reduced by the 1992 actions, the dollar asset risk premium would rise as investors shifted toward European assets.

Now we consider an increase in σ_f, holding all r's constant. From (30) we have the differential:

$$(32) \qquad \frac{\partial D}{\partial \sigma_f} = Rb \, \frac{\partial A}{\partial \sigma_f} - w(R-1) \left(\frac{\partial Z}{\partial \sigma_f} - \frac{\partial Z^*}{\partial \sigma_f} \right) - \frac{\partial C^*}{\partial \sigma_f} - R \frac{\partial Z^*}{\partial \sigma_f}.$$

From the definitions of the terms A, Z, Z^*, C, and C^*,

$$\frac{\partial A}{\partial \sigma_f} = 2(\sigma_f + \sigma_e \, r_{ef} - \sigma_b \, r_{bf});$$

$$\frac{\partial Z}{\partial \sigma_f} = 2\sigma_f - \sigma_b \, r_{bf} + 2\sigma_e \, r_{ef} - \sigma_p \, r_{pf};$$

$$(33) \qquad \frac{\partial Z^*}{\partial \sigma_f} = 2\sigma_f - \sigma_b r_{bf} + \sigma_e r_{ef} - \sigma_p^* r_{p*f};$$

---

13. This implicitly assumes that the absolute values of all correlation coefficients involving the return in the foreign assets are reduced.

$$\frac{\partial C}{\partial \sigma_f} = -\sigma_e \, r_{ef} + \sigma_p r_{pf};$$

$$\frac{\partial C^*}{\partial \sigma_f} = \sigma_p^* \, r_{p*f}.$$

Inserting the relations in (33) into (32) and gathering terms yields

$$\frac{\partial D}{\partial \sigma_f} = 2R(b-1)\sigma_f - R(2b-1)\sigma_b \, r_{bf}$$

(34)
$$+ [R(2b-1) - w(R-1)] \, \sigma_e \, r_{ef}$$

$$+ w(R-1) \, \sigma_p \, r_{pf} + [(R-1)(1-w)] \, \sigma_p^* \, r_{p*f}.$$

Note that if all r's (and therefore ρ's) are zero, (34) for $\partial D/\partial \sigma_f$ is equivalent to (31) for $\partial D/\partial \sigma_f^2$, holding all ρ's constant. The signs of the coefficients in (33) are as follows:

$$2R(b-1) < 0;$$

$$R(2b-1) \text{ depends on } b \gtrless \frac{1}{2};$$

$$[R(2b-1) - w(R-1)] \text{ negative if } b \leq \frac{1}{2};$$

$$w(R-1) > 0;$$

$$[(R-1)(1-w)] > 0; \text{ all assuming } R > 1.$$

The negative sign for the term in σ_f and the uncertain sign for the term in $\sigma_e \, r_{ef}$ are consistent with the results for $\partial \lambda/\partial \sigma_f$ in equation (19) and $\partial \lambda^*/\partial \sigma_f$ in equation (25). The overall result depends on the signs of the correlation coefficients. We make the following assumptions:

1. $r_{bp}, r_{fp}^* > 0$; nominal returns are positively correlated with own inflation.
2. $r_{ep} > 0$; $r_{ep}^* < 0$; devaluation raises the domestic price level and lowers the foreign.
3. $r_{eb} < 0$; $r_{ef} > 0$; a shift in the return differential toward F generates a depreciation.
4. $r_{bf}, r_{fp}, r_{bp}^* \approx 0$.

With these presumptions, the second and fourth terms in (34) become approximately zero, the first is negative, the fifth is positive, and the third is unclear but likely to be negative. The positive term in r_{p*f} represents the reduction in risk on the real return on F as the covariance of $P*$ and the F return rises.

The uncertainty regarding the term in $\sigma_e \, r_{ef}$ arises from the possibility that $R(2b-1)$ is positive. The $2b$ term appears because the overall variance term RA is in the denominator of both λ and $\lambda*$, so an increase in σ_f reduces λ and $\lambda*$ by increasing A. This alone would require an increase in D to maintain equilibrium. This is offset by the positive effects through Z and $Z*$ in the numerators of λ and $\lambda*$. Thus, is it likely that the term in $\sigma_e r_{ef}$ is negative; it is sufficient that $b=0.5$.

Thus, the general conclusion in the case of identical information is that a reduction in riskiness of one asset shifts asset demands toward that asset, increasing the risk premium in the other asset. The quantitative effects are given by equations (21) and (34) in our two cases, which are the same if all p_{fi} terms are zero.

Market Equilibrium with Asymmetric Biased Information

The experiments above assumed that information about the volatility of the returns on the foreign asset improved identically for all investors. In this section we ask what happens to the uncovered differential D if information improves for only one set of investors. Specifically, we assume that home and foreign investors may have different estimates of the variance of the returns on F; the home investor's σ_f^2 differs from the foreign investor's σ_f^{*2}.

This would be the case, for example, if the foreign investor had better information on his home assets than the home investor has. A reduction in σ_f^2 would represent an improvement in home investors' information about foreign assets. This could be a result, for example, of the integration of European financial markets in 1992. Non-European investors might acquire better (or cheaper) information about European assets with no compensating change in the knowledge available to Europeans on non-European assets.

The procedure we follow is first to write the market equilibrium condition for D, and then to calculate $\partial D / \partial \sigma_f^2$, holding σ_f^{*2} and all covariances constant. This is equivalent to the first experiment above, but assumes that only the home investor's information changes. This experiment can be interpreted as a movement away from the identical information equilibrium if we begin with $\sigma_f^2 = \sigma_f^{*2}$, and then change only σ_f^2.

In this case, with $\sigma_f^2 \neq \sigma_f^{*2}$, A and A^* differ, as well as C and C^* and Z and Z^*. So the equilibrium condition, from equation (29), is now

$$(35) \qquad b = \frac{1}{RA}[D+C+RZ]w + \frac{1}{RA^*}[D+C^*+RZ^*](1-w).$$

Note here that since $A \neq A^*$ we cannot linearize the solution, as before, and that we could easily assume $R \neq R^*$ without further complicating the analysis. We consider a change in information to be more interesting than a change in the taste for risk.

If we isolate the terms in D in equation (35), we obtain

$$(36) \qquad b = D\left[\frac{w}{RA} + \frac{1-w}{RA^*}\right] + w\frac{C+RZ}{RA} + (1-w)\frac{C^*+RZ^*}{RA^*}.$$

The home perception of riskiness of return on the foreign asset σ_f^2 enters only in A and Z, with $\partial A/\partial \sigma_f^2 = \partial Z/\partial \sigma_f^2 = 1$. We can totally differentiate (36), allowing D and σ_f^2 to change, use the solution for λ in a substitution, and solve for $dD/d\sigma_f^2$ to obtain the result:

$$(37) \qquad \frac{dD}{d\sigma_f^2} = \frac{\dfrac{w}{A}(\lambda - 1)}{\left(\dfrac{w}{RA} + \dfrac{1-w}{RA^*}\right)} < 0.$$

The numerator is negative and the denominator positive.

This result is intuitively clear. Given σ_f^{*2}, an *increase* in σ_f^2 drives home investors toward the home asset, reducing D. The expression for $\partial \lambda/\partial \sigma_f$ in (19) shows the shift in demand for the home asset. But $\partial \lambda^*/\partial \sigma_f^2 = 0$, since σ_f^{*2}, not σ_f^2, enters the foreign investor's demand functions. So only home investors shift home in this case, while in the case of identical information all investors shift toward the home asset.

A decrease in σ_f^2, representing an improvement in home investors' information about foreign assets, would increase D, raising the home interest rate i_d relative to the foreign rate i_f. Thus, one implication of the European financial reforms of 1992 might be to reduce interest rates (and the cost of capital) in Europe relative to outside Europe.

Next we turn to the case where σ_f changes, holding all r's constant. This is the equivalent of the second experiment earlier, but with only the home investor's demand functions shifting. Terms in σ_f or ρ_{fi} enter A, C, and Z in equation (36); their derivatives with respect to σ_f are given in equation (33). We totally differentiate equation (36), allowing D and σ_f to change holding all r_{fi}'s constant, use the solution for λ in a substitution, substitute the expressions in (32) for $\partial A/\partial\sigma_f$, $\partial Z/\partial\sigma_f$, and $\partial C/\partial\sigma_f$ to obtain the following result:

$$(38) \qquad \frac{dD}{d\sigma_f} = -\frac{N}{\left(\dfrac{w}{RA} + \dfrac{1-w}{RA^*}\right)} \gtreqless 0 \text{ as } N \gtreqless -0,$$

where:

$$N = \frac{w}{A}\left\{ 2(1-\lambda)\sigma_f + (2\lambda-1)\sigma_b\, r_{bf} + [2(1-\lambda) - \frac{1}{R}]\sigma_e\, r_{ef} \right.$$
$$\left. - \left(1-\frac{1}{R}\right)\sigma_p\, r_{pf}\right\} = w\frac{\partial\lambda}{\partial\sigma_f},$$

and $\partial\lambda/\partial\sigma_f$ is given in equation (19) earlier. Note that, as in the case of identical information, if all r's were zero, equation (38) would be equivalent to (37).

Since only the home investor's demands shift in this case, the home demand shift is in the numerator of $\partial D/\partial\sigma_f$. The direct effect via σ_f is to reduce D as σ_f rises, as before. The effect via the $\sigma_e\, r_{ef}$ term is uncertain, as discussed earlier. Since $R > 1$, $\lambda < 0.5$ is sufficient for this covariance effect to be positive.

Market Equilibrium with Symmetric Biased Information

The last case we examine is one in which both sets of investors are assumed to have better information about their home assets than the foreign assets. This is a symmetric version of the case just discussed. We assume that it is possible that $\sigma_f \neq \sigma_f^*$ and $\sigma_b \neq \sigma_b^*$, where the starred versions are the foreign investor's estimates of the riskiness of returns. In this framework we can examine the effect of a symmetric change in perceived risk by changing σ_f and σ_b^*, holding σ_f^* and σ_b constant. We assume the changes in σ_f and σ_b^* are equal to a common $d\sigma$. We then solve for the effects on D in equation (36) in the two cases in which (a) all relevant ρ's are held constant and (b) all r's are held constant.

Since the total differentiation of (36) effectively linearizes it, we would expect the case of a change in symmetrically biased information to add a term in the foreign demand shift to the numerators in the expressions in equations (37) and (38) in the case of one-sided bias, with the opposite sign. This is indeed the case.

First, we note that the terms in $d\sigma_f$ will enter the differentials of A, C, and Z in equation (36), and the terms in $d\sigma_b^*$ will enter the differentials of A^*, C^*, and Z^*. Totally differentiating (36), allowing D, σ_f^2, and σ_b^{*2} to change, holding all relevant ρ's constant, yields

$$(39) \qquad \frac{dD}{d\sigma^2} = \frac{\dfrac{w}{A}(\lambda - 1) + \dfrac{1-w}{A^*}(\lambda^*)}{\left(\dfrac{w}{RA} + \dfrac{1-w}{RA^*}\right)}.$$

Here the two demand shifts have offsetting effects on D. With a symmetric increase in perceived riskiness of the foreign return, both sets of investors shift toward the home asset. So the sign of the numerator in (39) depends on the net effect of the two shifts. If the entire model is symmetric, with $A = A^*$, $w = 1 - w$, and $(1 - \lambda) = \lambda^*$, then $dD/d\sigma^2$ in (39) is zero.

Turning to the case where all relevant r's are held constant, we must first write the partial derivatives of A^*, C^*, and Z^* with respect to σ_b^*, noting that in their previous definitions σ_b is replaced by σ_b^*:

$$(40) \qquad \begin{aligned} \frac{\partial A^*}{\partial \sigma_b^*} &= 2\sigma_b - 2\sigma_f\, r_{bf}^* - 2\sigma_e r_{ef}^*; \\[2mm] \frac{\partial C^*}{\partial \sigma_b^*} &= -\sigma_e\, r_{eb}^* - \sigma_p^*\, r_{bp^*}^*; \\[2mm] \frac{\partial Z^*}{\partial \sigma_b^*} &= -\sigma_f\, r_{bf}^* + \sigma_p^*\, r_{bp^*}^*. \end{aligned}$$

Now to obtain the solution for $\partial D/\partial \sigma$, we totally differentiate (36) allowing A, A^*, C, C^*, Z, Z^*, and D to change, and then substitute from (33) for $\partial A^*/\partial \sigma_b^*$, and so forth to obtain

$$(41) \qquad \frac{dD}{d\sigma} = -\frac{w\dfrac{\partial \lambda}{\partial \sigma_f} + (1-w)\dfrac{\partial \lambda^*}{\partial \sigma_b}}{\left(\dfrac{w}{RA} + \dfrac{1-w}{RA^*}\right)},$$

where $\partial \lambda/\partial \sigma_f$ is given by equation (19), likely to be positive, and $\partial \lambda^*/\partial \sigma_b$ is given by equation (26), likely to be negative.

Although it is not obvious from the form in which (41) is written, if all r's are assumed to be zero, it is equivalent to (39). Again, the two demand shifts have offsetting effects. It is obvious in (41) that if $w = (1 - w)$ and the two demand partials were equal in size, the effect on D would be zero. But this is not likely to be the case, because the terms in the two partials are not the same. But the general result from the cases of biased information is that a one-sided improvement moves the investor with the improvement toward that asset, reducing its relative expected return, while the effects are offsetting with a two-sided improvement.

4. CONCLUSIONS: THE EFFECTS OF IMPROVING INFORMATION

We can now summarize our main conclusions concerning the influence of information on portfolio decisions. A change in information always has the direct effect, of course, of causing investors in each of the countries to alter their portfolio decisions. But this is only the starting point for analyzing the effects of changing information. For one thing, by aggregating investor demand across countries, the effects of changing information on home asset preference and on security risk premiums can also be deduced. For another thing, if access to information varies by country, then changes in information will have differential effects on investors in different countries.

We assume in all cases that there are two countries—a *home country* and a *foreign country*—each with a single risky investment asset. There then ensues an improvement in information regarding investments in the foreign asset (the asset in the foreign country). We focus in this section on the case in which the improvement in information reduces the variance of the return on the foreign asset, while all covariances involving the foreign asset remain fixed.[14] In Section 3 we derived comparable results for special cases, given that the variance and covariance terms vary in proportion.[15]

We now summarize the results of a series of cases in which investors have varying amounts of access to information changes.

---

14. If the foreign asset variance changes while its covariances are constant, then all the correlation coefficients involving the foreign asset must be changing.

15. In this case, the correlation coefficients must be constant. Constant correlation coefficients and constant covariance terms yield the same result if the correlation coefficients are all zero, or if the correlation coefficients meet the other sufficient conditions identified in Section 3.

Identical Access to Information

We first consider the case in which all investors have identical access to information, so that the reduced risk of the foreign asset is equally apparent to all of them. The direct result is that investors in both countries allocate a larger share of their portfolios to the foreign asset, as can be seen in equations (18) and (24). Since the improved information raises the demand for the foreign asset, it will also reduce the foreign asset risk premium—the sum of the nominal return on the foreign asset and the expected depreciation of the home currency minus the nominal return on the home asset—as shown in equation (31).

The size of the increase in demand for each group of investors is proportional, moreover, to the portfolio share initially allocated to the foreign asset.[16] Consequently, if home asset preference is zero initially— portfolio shares are the same for home and foreign investors—then the change in information does not affect home asset preference. Alternatively, if home asset preference is positive—the foreign asset share is higher for foreign investors than for home investors—then home asset preference will rise as foreign asset information improves.

Asymmetric Access to Information

As a second case, it is assumed that the home and foreign investors have differential access to information regarding the foreign asset. In particular, in Section 3 we examined the case in which home country investors, and only home country investors, observe an improvement in foreign asset information. This could correspond, for example, to a case in which better information regarding European securities becomes available to non-European investors.

The direct result is again that the relevant investors—only the home-country investors in this case—increase the share of their portfolios allocated to the foreign asset. The demand by foreign investors does not change since, by assumption, there is no change in the information available to them. Given that foreign asset demand rises overall, the foreign asset risk premium will fall, just as it did in the case of identical information (see equation (37)). Of course, the magnitude of the change in

16. For example, from equation (18) it is easy to see that $d(1 - \lambda)/d\sigma_f^2 = -(1/A)(1 - \lambda)$.

the risk premium will be limited, because the change in information is assumed to affect only one group of investors.

Since only the foreign asset demand of home country investors rises, the information change also has the effect of reducing the magnitude of home asset preference. For example, if home asset preference were initially positive, then it would fall as home-country investors allocate a larger share of their portfolios to the foreign asset.

Symmetric But Biased Access to Information

As the third case, it is assumed that both home and foreign investors receive improved information, but regarding only the assets of their own country: the home asset for home investors, and the foreign asset for foreign investors. The result is that home investor demand shifts toward the home asset, whereas foreign investor demand shifts toward the foreign asset. Home asset preference thus unambiguously increases. Moreover, the two shifts in demand occur in opposite directions, so if they are also equal in magnitude, there will be no net effect on equilibrium risk premiums. This is a good illustration of the complex manner in which information can interact with real interest rate spreads.

Applications to "Europe 1992"

In using these results to analyze "Europe 1992," the most relevant case would appear to be an asymmetric change in information, in which home-country investors (non-Europeans) observe a decline in the riskiness of foreign (European) assets. As we have just seen, the result should be an increase in demand and a reduction in the risk premiums with regard to European securities. The beneficiaries of this change would include both non-European investors and European borrowers (issuers of securities).

The overall results of "Europe 1992," however, may be more complex than this simple, direct effect suggests. For example, non-European investors may be surprised to find that improved information results in lower, not higher, expected returns on European securities. In other words, the benefits of reduced uncertainty may seem subtle compared to the reduction in expected returns caused by the demand shift. The complex nature of evaluating welfare effects when information changes is also illustrated in the paper by Bruce Miller and Thomas Copeland, "The Welfare Effects of Public Information in an Asymmetric Information Market,'' which also appears in this symposium.

More generally, the information changes created by "Europe 1992" may be the source of a variety of additional effects, some of which we can now examine. An immediate point is that a change in risk premium levels creates losers as well as gainers. For example, as the risk premiums on European securities fall, European investors will earn lower returns on their local investments. European investors will thus lose some or all of the excess return they had been earning as a result of their informational advantage.

Accounting for gainers and losers will become even more complex to the extent that European investors will also gain from improved *intra-European* information. For example, French investors may obtain better information with regard to Spanish investments. Consequently, a French investor will benefit from improved information regarding his non-French European investments, even while he is losing with regard to French investments.

Another factor is that the improvements in information may be restricted to certain classes of European securities. For example, additional information may become available primarily for publicly traded debt and equity securities, where uniform accounting and reporting standards are relevant. In contrast, changes of this form are unlikely to create benefits for bank loans that are originated in local markets and held by local banks.[17] Nevertheless, interest rates on bank loans may still decline, assuming that "Europe 1992" encourages entry by foreign banks into local markets as part of banking industry deregulation.

The changes created by "Europe 1992" may even *increase* the riskiness of certain European securities. A particularly intriguing possibility is that the government bonds of European countries may become risky as these countries lose their autonomy with regard to monetary and fiscal policy. In this case, the government bonds of European countries would be similar to the bonds issued by various state governments within the United States. The result, of course, would be an increase in the interest rates for these securities.

The Role of Information for Real Interest Spreads

This paper began by noting that real interest rate levels in countries could vary as the result of risk premiums. Although the finance literature

---

17. See Jaffee and Stiglitz (1989) for a discussion of the informational aspects of bank lending.

has focused on such factors as unequal distributions for wealth and securities, or different consumption preferences, as the source of real interest rate spreads, we have shown that imperfect information may be an equally important source of these rate spreads.

In particular, an improvement in information will generally be reflected in reduced real interest rate spreads. Although such changes are usually beneficial, there will be a distribution of gainers and losers. With regard to "Europe 1992," for example, the reduction in real interest rate spreads will also reflect, among other things, a reduction in the ability of European central banks to control their domestic interest rates through monetary policy.

APPENDIX

1. Purchasing Power Parity

Purchasing power parity requires that the exchange rate equal the ratio of the price levels of the two countries:

(a.1) $$E = \frac{P}{P*}$$

The dynamic process for the exchange rate is then

(a.2) $$dE = \frac{dP}{P*} - \frac{P\ dP*}{P*^2} - \frac{dP\ dP*}{P*^2} - \frac{P\ dP*^2}{P*^3},$$

which can be rewritten using (a.1) as

(a.3) $$\frac{dE}{E} = \frac{dP}{P} - \frac{dP*}{P*} - \frac{dP\ dP*}{P\ P*} - \left[\frac{dP*}{P*}\right]^2,$$

Making substitutions based on equations (11) to (13) yields

(a.4) $$\pi_e\ dt + \sigma_e dz_e = (\pi_p\ dt + \sigma_p\ dz_p) - (\pi_p^*\ dt + \sigma_p^*\ dz_p^*) - (\rho_{pp}^*\ dt) - \sigma_{p*}^2 dt.$$

Ex ante purchasing power parity holds when the expected changes in (a.4) (i.e., the terms in *dt*) are equal:

(a.5) $$\pi_e = \pi_p - \pi_p^* - \rho_{pp}^* - \sigma_{p^*}^2.$$

Ex post purchasing power parity holds when, in addition, the stochastic terms in (a.4) are equal:

$$\sigma_e \, dz_e = \sigma_p \, dz_p - \sigma_p^* \, dz_p^*.$$

Multiplying through by $\sigma_e dz_e$, we then have

(a.6) $$\sigma_e^2 = \rho_{ep} - \rho_{ep}^*,$$

where ρ_{ep} and ρ_{ep^*} are the covariances of P and P^* respectively with respect to the exchange rate.

2. Uncovered Interest Rate Parity

Uncovered interest rate parity (UIP) requires that

(a.7) $$\frac{dB}{B} = \frac{dF}{F} + \frac{dE}{E}.$$

Making substitutions based on equations (9) to (11) we have

(a.8) $$i_b \, dt + \sigma_b \, dz_b = i_f + \sigma_f \, dz_f + (\pi_e + \rho_{ef}) \, dt + \sigma_e \, dz_e.$$

Ex ante UIP requires that the expected terms in equation (a.8) be equal:

(a.9) $$i_b - i_f - \pi_e - \rho_{ef} = 0.$$

Ex post UIP requires, in addition, that the stochastic terms in (a.8) be equal:

$$\sigma_b \, dz_b = \sigma_f \, dz_f + \sigma_e \, dz_e.$$

Multiplying through by $\sigma_e dz_e$, we then have:

(a.10) $$\sigma_e^2 - \rho_{eb} + \rho_{ef} = 0.$$

REFERENCES

Adler, Michael, and Bernard Dumas. 1983. "International Portfolio Choice and Corporation Finance: A Synthesis." *Journal of Finance* 38 (3), 925–984.

Adler, Michael, and Bruce Lehmann. 1983. "Deviations from Purchasing Power Parity in the Long Run." *Journal of Finance* 38 (4), 1471–1487.

Barry, Christopher B., and Stephen J. Brown. 1985. "Differential Information and Security Market Equilibrium." *Journal of Financial and Quantitative Analysis* 20 (4), 407–422.

Bawa, Vijay S., Stephen J. Brown, and Roger W. Klein. 1979. *Estimation Risk and Optimal Portfolio Choice.* North-Holland Publishing Company.

Black, Fischer. 1974. "International Capital Market Equilibrium with Investment Barriers." *Journal of Financial Economics* 1 (3), 337–352.

Branson, William H., and Dale Henderson. 1985. "The Specification and Influence of Asset

Markets." In R. W. Jones and P. B. Kenen (eds.), *Handbook of International Economics*, Vol. 2. Elsevier Science Publishers.

Brown, S. 1979. "The Effect of Estimation Risk on Capital Market Equilibrium." *Journal of Financial and Quantitative Analysis* 14 (2), 215–220.

Fraga, Arminio. 1986. "Price Uncertainty and the Exchange-Rate Risk Premium." *Journal of International Economics* 20, 179–185.

Frankel, Jeffrey A. 1989. "Quantifying International Capital Mobility in the 1980s." NBER Working Paper No. 2856.

Frankel, Jeffrey A., and Alan T. MacArthur. 1988. "Political vs. Currency Premia in International Real Interest Differentials." *European Economic Review* 32, 1083–1121.

Frenkel, Jacob A. 1981. "Flexible Exchange Rates, Prices and the Role of 'News': Lessons from the 1970s." *Journal of Political Economy* 89 (6), 665–705.

Grossman, Sanford J., and Joseph E. Stiglitz. 1980. "On the Impossibility of Informationally Efficient Markets." *American Economic Review* 70 (June), 393–408.

Ho, Thomas S. Y., and Roni Michaely. 1988. "Information Quality and Market Efficiency." *Journal of Financial and Quantitative Analysis* 23 (1), 53–70.

Jaffee, Dwight M., and Joseph Stiglitz. 1990. "Credit Rationing." In Benjamin Friedman (ed.), *Handbook in Financial Economics*. North-Holland Publishing Company.

Merton, Robert C. 1987. "A Simple Model of Capital Market Equilibrium with Incomplete Information." *Journal of Finance* 42 (3), 483–510.

Obstfeld, Maurice. 1986. "Capital Mobility in the World Economy: Theory and Measurement." *Carnegie-Rochester Series on Public Policy* 24 (Spring), 55–103.

Stein, Jeremy C. 1987. "Informational Externalities and Welfare-Reducing Speculation." *Journal of Political Economy* 95 (6), 1123–1145.

Stulz, Rene M. 1981. "On the Effects of Barriers to International Investment," *Journal of Finance* 36 (4), 923–934.

Comments

MICHAEL ADLER*

Branson and Jaffee's (B&J) paper performs two signal services. First, it provides a useful survey and synthesis of the various ways that incomplete information can affect portfolio decisions and equilibrium return–risk relationships. Second, properly read, the paper offers a fairly comprehensive list of the generally very strong assumptions that are required before one can extract unambiguously the results of a change in the quality of information. Let me dwell briefly on this second aspect.

In my view, the problem is but another manifestation of the former of two fundamental difficulties confronting the field, apparent also in the companion paper by Adler and Prasad. One is that reductions in the variances of assets' returns distributions generally can be accompanied by unpredictable changes in off-diagonal elements of the variance–covariance matrix. In equilibrium, there is a presumption that changes in the quality of information will simultaneously affect all elements of the variance–covariance matrix. Computed portfolio weights may therefore acquire the wrong signs unless the requisite restrictions on variances and covariances are empirically valid. The other, not an issue in B&J's one-period approach, is that the direction of investors' intertemporal hedging behavior cannot be determined for most utility functions. It is therefore not surprising that the effects of incomplete information on capital flows have not heretofore been closely studied, as B&J observe. It seems clear that for the time being the most interesting and empirically relevant cases rapidly become intractable.

These considerations lead me to the provisional conclusion that a putative informational improvement, partly captured by reduced parameter uncertainty of the B&J variety, is unlikely either to be modeled the most easily or, for that matter, to be the most important cause of shifts in the pattern of capital flows between the United States and Europe in the 1990s. Improved financial reporting standards may not have the effects summarized by the sufficient conditions associated with equations (18), (19), (24), and (25). Any change in the quality of information is likely

*Graduate School of Business, Columbia University.

to reach Europeans and non-Europeans simultaneously. The effects of changes in the quality of information are going to be hard to isolate, quite aside from their being theoretically indeterminate. It seems to me that one might well look to changes in barriers other than informational imperfections as alternative and possibly equally promising sources of propositions regarding capital flows.

These things said, Branson and Jaffee's paper offers further implications for future research of a somewhat more detailed, technical nature. Their attempt to introduce information-quality considerations into the theory of capital flows is likely to draw others behind them. Let me spell out a few of the more obvious issues.

From among alternative parameter uncertainty models, B&J chose the one where improved information reduces variances without changing expected returns. Tractability is presumably the justification for this selection, though no reason is given. Those who follow may prefer to choose differently. For one thing, portfolio choice models are empirically much more sensitive to estimation risk on the means than on the variances of expected returns. For another, the static approach of the paper rules out learning. Moreover, the static model forces everyone to behave intertemporally as if his utility function were logarithmic. Future researchers may find this imposition of myopia to be unduly restrictive.

Future researchers may also want to expand the menu of assets. For most of their paper B&J inexplicably omit nominally riskless assets. Later they contrast cases where all assets are either riskless or risky. If one assumes only riskless assets together with *ex post* purchasing power parity (PPP)—or only risky assets, nonstochastic inflation, and uncovered interest rate parity (UIP)—the world contains effectively but one asset. It is no surprise that home-asset preference (HAP) disappears in either setting, as B&J find. Risky and riskless assets should feature together. One way to obtain HAP meaningfully is to allow for different stochastic inflation rates, PPP deviations, and one nominally riskless asset per country. Perhaps a more complete specification would also help one penetrate the interpretation of D, actually the difference between the expected returns on two risky securities, which is given here as the equilibrium (exchange risk?) risk premium.

Finally, there is the necessary work of verifying the empirical validity of the many assumptions that B&J had to make. The news may not be altogether bad if some are found not to hold. Although clearcut theoretical propositions may well disappear, numerical simulations may still prove productive for policy purposes.

Optimal Foreign Currency Hedging When Information Is Imperfect

MICHAEL ADLER* AND BHASKAR PRASAD*

I. INTRODUCTION

This paper presents a limited attempt at incorporating into currency hedging theory the growing evidence that the forward risk premium is unobservable and random, but perhaps with a tendency to revert toward zero. This is largely impossible in the usual hedging model, which assumes that investors are certain about the parameters of the spot and futures exchange rate processes. We are concerned with several of the effects and implications of this extension: on investors' demands for forward exchange positions as portfolio assets; for the speculative and hedging behavior of individual investors; and for the possibility that a concept of equilibrium hedging can usefully be characterized.

Our technical point of departure is to allow the forward risk premium— that is, the mean of the change in the futures price—to follow a zero-mean-reverting diffusion process. As the risk premium can no longer be observed directly, it must be estimated. In our current approach, the investor gives the risk premium a normal prior density and uses a Kalman–Bucy filter to update his prior.

The main effect of letting the risk premium be exogenously random in Section II is to make it function like any state variable. It gives rise to an additional Merton–Breeden hedging term in the investor's optimal asset demand functions. These demand equations, decomposed, enable us to comment critically on recent claims (cf. Perold and Schulman, 1988) that all international portfolios should be fully and permanently hedged against foreign currency risk.

When information is imperfect, investors modify their behavior de-

*The authors are professor and doctoral candidate, respectively, at the Graduate School of Business, Columbia University.

They would like, without implicating them, to thank Edwin Elton and Jerome Detemple for their critical comments.

pending on how well they expect to forecast the risk premium on the average over time and how precisely they do so at any point. Section III shows that an investor's effective speculation may, but need not, increase as both his forecasting ability and his precision improve. As the signs of the intertemporal hedging terms are generally ambiguous, imperfect information need not be accompanied by greater cautiousness. What is more, revising his forecasts using the Kalman–Bucy filter is similar to following a technical trading rule, a class of behavior that is ruled out in existing, perfect information, intertemporal CAPMs.

Section IV studies the possible existence of universal hedge ratios that are the same across investors of different nationalities. The set of all such ratios is spelled out. Imperfect information, even if it is shared equally across countries, unfortunately but unsurprisingly makes hedging ratios generally different unless investors' endowments and utility functions are identical. Section V concludes.

II. MODELING ASSET DEMANDS WITH IMPERFECT INFORMATION

Optimal asset demands with unobservable state variables have been studied by Detemple (1986), Gennotte (1986), and Dothan and Feldman (1986). In this section we employ their methodology to investigate how the unobservability of the forward risk premium affects international portfolio hedging decisions.

Because equity securities have no intrinsic currency denomination, we are free for present purposes to treat all domestic and foreign stocks as if they traded in a single location. All are then priced in a common currency, say $U.S. Their price variations are given by the diffusion:

(1) $$dA_t = A[\mu_a(Z,t)dt + \sigma_a dz_a],$$

where dA is an $(N \times 1)$ vector of $U.S. price changes; A is a diagonal matrix whose diagonal is the vector of $U.S. prices, μ_a is the state-dependent vector of mean rates of return, $V_{aa} = \rho\sigma_a'\sigma_a$ is the variance–covariance matrix, and z_a is a vector Wiener process. We assume that the investor has certainty regarding the parameters of the process.[1]

The observable-state variable follows the process:

1. In short, we treat risk premiums in the capital and foreign exchange markets asymmetrically

(2) $$dZ = \mu_z(Z,t)dt + \sigma_z dz_z.$$

In addition, there are L foreign exchange forward contracts, each written on one of the spot exchange rates. Exchange rates are quoted in U.S. terms (that is, \$U.S./FC), where FC stands for foreign currency.[2] The forward contracts promise delivery at time T of a fixed amount of spot exchange at a forward price fixed at time 0. They are marked to market (i.e., in effect rewritten) continuously on a discounted basis, leaving their net value equal to zero at any instant. The $(L \times 1)$ vector of settlement prices, F_t, satisfies the stochastic differential equation:

(3) $$dF_t = F(\mu_f dt + \sigma_f dz_f)$$

where F and σ_f are known and dF can be observed.

The mean of dF/F in equation (3), μ_f, is the unobservable risk premium, which is replaced by a forecast, below. Under standard no-arbitrage conditions, $\mu_f = \mu_s - (r - r^*)$, where μ_s is the expected spot exchange rate change and $(r - r^*)$ is the differential between the domestic and foreign nominal interest rates. Were the spot rate an exact driftfree martingale, $\mu_s = 0$; and $\mu_f = r^* - r$ would be observable. There is a large body of empirical evidence to the effect that the spot rate is most nearly a sub- or super-martingale with an unobservable, possibly fluctuating, nonzero drift. Efforts to extract the forward risk premium directly have produced certain stylized facts.[3] The unconditional risk premium, estimated as an average in long time series over many periods, often seems to converge on zero. However, the conditional risk premium (that is, the risk premium for short holding periods of three months or less) apparently fluctuates between positive and negative values and is seldom actually zero. Conditional risk premiums, which

in what follows, assuming the former to be known, whereas the latter are not. However, our purpose at this stage is neither total descriptive realism nor full consistency with general equilibrium. Some justification of our approach can be inferred from Giovannini and Jorion (1989). Empirically the two risk premiums behave quite differently. The unconditional U.S. capital market risk premium is significantly greater than zero; and it is hard to improve on a constant for the specification of the conditional U.S. market risk premium.

2. Forward contracts are zero-investment combinations of foreign and domestic bonds. As all fixed-income instruments and forward contracts have equal maturities, forward exchange contracts replace foreign bonds in the asset menu; and they are priced by arbitrage even when interest rates are random, unlike futures.

3. The literature on this topic is vast. Some of the better known papers are Fama (1984), Domowitz and Hakkio (1985), Giovannini and Jorion (1987), Wolff (1987), and Giovannini and Jorion (1989).

can remain on either side of zero for lengthy but varying periods of time, also appear to be serially correlated.[4]

These considerations lead us to suggest that the vector of risk premiums can plausibly be modeled by the process:

$$(4) \qquad d\mu_f = -k\mu_f dt + \sigma_\mu dz_\mu,$$

where only k and σ_μ are known. Note that $k < 0$ makes no sense as $\text{var}(\mu_{f,t+dt}|\mu_{ft})$ tends to a negative number. We constrain k to be positive. Values of $k > 0$ make the risk premiums, zero-mean-reverting processes. When $k = 0$, μ_f is a pure martingale.[5]

As the forward risk premium is unobservable, it must be estimated. At time t the investor forecasts a Gaussian prior distribution for the μ_f, with mean vector, μ_f^+, and estimated variance, σ_e^+; that is, he forecasts

$$(5) \qquad \mu_f = \mu_f^+ + e,$$

where the forecasting error is distributed $N(0, \sigma_e^+)$. As the true value of μ_f in (5) is unobservable, so also is the true variance, σ_e. The investor therefore uses σ_e^+—an estimate. Over the interval $(t, t+dt)$ he observes dF/F_t which is known to be correlated with $d\mu_f$.[6] The dual assumptions, that dF/F and $d\mu_f$ are linearly dependent on μ_f and that σ_μ is independent of μ_f, cause the conditional distribution, $\mu_{ft}|F_t^y$, where $F_t^y = \{F_s : 0 \leq s \leq t\}$, also to be Gaussian (Lipster and Shiryayev, 1977). The first two moments are therefore sufficient to characterize the entire distribution.

Following Lipster and Shiryayev, the optimal nonlinear filter, which minimizes the mean-squared error, provides the updated conditional moments at $(t + dt)$. These updated conditional moments are the moments at t plus the revisions given below due to observing F_{t+dt}:

---

4. This autocorrelation is presumably related to the widely shared observation that interest rate levels are strongly serially correlated.

5. Equation (4) is known as the Ornstein–Uhlenbeck constant elasticity of variance process. When μ_f is normally distributed, it has the properties that:

$$E(\mu_{f,t+dt}|\mu_{ft}) = \mu_{ft}[\exp(-k\tau)]; \text{ and } \text{var}(\mu_{f,t+dt}|\mu_{ft}) = (\sigma_\mu^2/2k)[1 - \exp(-2k\tau)].$$

It has the double implication that, as $\tau \to \infty$, the long-run mean approaches zero; and that the steady state variance tends to $(\sigma_\mu^2/2k)$, which falls as k rises.

6. Our specification is equivalent to that of Detemple (1986), as the relationship between the two Wiener processes, dz_f and dz_μ, is fixed by our parameters. Note that $\text{cov}(dF/F, d\mu_f) = \rho\sigma_\mu\sigma_f$ and is known if ρ is known. To emphasize the distinction between true and predicted quantities, we write $\sigma_{f\mu}^+ = \text{cov}(dF/F, d\mu_f^+)$ in what follows.

$$(6) \qquad d\mu_f^+ = -k\mu_f^+ dt + [(\rho\sigma_\mu\sigma_f + \sigma_e^+)/\sigma_f^2] \left(\frac{dF}{F} - \mu_f^+ dt\right)$$

$$(7) \qquad d\sigma_e^+ = (-2k\sigma_e^+ + \sigma_\mu^2)dt - [(\rho\sigma_\mu\sigma_f + \sigma_e^+)^2/\sigma_f^2]dt.$$

Equation (6) tells us that μ_f^+, the expected value of the conditional forecast, changes stochastically through time. Equation (7) reflects the known outcome that when the prior density of μ_f is normal, the conditional variance of the forecast moves deterministically through time.

We now turn to the derivation of optimal asset demands. Being rational, investors evaluate future returns in real terms, that is, after deflating nominal returns by their idiosyncratic price index, denoted I for inflation. We assume that inflation follows the process:[7]

$$(8) \qquad dI = \mu_i(I,t)dt + \sigma_i(I,t)dz_i.$$

As inflation is stochastic, there is no asset that is riskless in real terms. Furthermore, although nominal interest rates must be random to account for the serial correlation in the risk premium, they are instantaneously known.[8] If the instantaneous interest rate on a domestic, nominally riskless short-term bond is r, the bond's real return is:

$$(9) \qquad R = (r - \mu_i/I + \sigma_i^2/I^2)dt - (\sigma_i/I)dz_i.$$

Nominal wealth accumulates when the returns on assets and forward contracts exceed outlays on current consumption. The intertemporal nominal wealth constraint is given by:

$$(10) \qquad dW = w'W(dA/A) + X'dF + [(1 - w'l)rW - C]dt,$$

where w is the $(N \times 1)$ vector of wealth fractions invested in each risky asset and w' is its transpose; X' is the $(1 \times L)$ vector of forward exchange positions in contracts that cost nothing to enter but pay off dF continuously thereafter; and C is the instantaneous consumption rate.

It is well known that in an incomplete-information world, agents sep-

---

7. The process for inflation is left very general to accommodate the potential problems marked by Adler and Dumas (1983, pp. 940–941). The issues relate to the consistent specification of endogenous price-index processes in an equilibrium when investors have heterogeneous consumption preferences.

8. For present purposes we have no need of explicit processes for interest rates. In equilibrium, interest rates should be endogenous, as in Cox, Ingersoll, and Ross (CIR) (1985). CIR's is a single-country model, however; extending it to two or more countries is a difficult problem for future research. In such an extension, the stochastic processes for interest rates would naturally be consistent with the diffusion assumed for the forward exchange rate.

arate the investment decision problem into two stages. First, they derive the updated unobservable parameters (the conditional risk premiums in our case). In the second stage they choose optimal portfolios using the conditional means instead of the unobservable risk premiums. This separation theorem, together with equations (1) to (4), enables us to write out (10) more fully as:

$$(11) \qquad dW = [w'W\mu_a + X'F\mu_f^+ + (1 - w'l)rW - C)]dt$$
$$+ w'W\sigma_a dz_a + X'F\sigma_f dz_f',$$

where $dz_f' = \{[(dF/F) - \mu_f^+ dt]/\sigma_f\}$, with $z_f'(0) = 0$, is the normalized deviation of the returns on a forward contract from its conditional mean.[9]

To go from nominal to real terms, we define real wealth as $Y = W/I$. After applying Ito's Lemma,

$$dY = [(w'W/I) (\mu_a - r - V_{ai}/I) + (X'F/I) (\mu_f^+ - V_{fi}/I)$$
$$(12) \qquad + (W/I) (r - \mu_i/I + \sigma_i^2/I^2) - C/I]dt$$
$$+ (w'W/I)\sigma_a dz_a + (X'F/I)\sigma_f dz_f' - (W/I^2)\sigma_i dz_i$$

where V_{ai} and V_{fi}, respectively, are vectors containing the covariances of the returns on risky assets and forward contracts with inflation. Each investor solves the program

$$(13) \qquad \underset{\{w'Y, X'F/I, C/I\}}{\text{Maximize E}} \int_t^T U(C/I, s)ds, \quad \text{subject to (12)}.$$

This enables us to write the Bellman equation, where μ_f^+ acts as a state variable, as:

---

9. By virtue of the definition, $dz_f' = [(1/\sigma_f)(dF/F - \mu_f^+ dt] = [(\mu_f - \mu_f^+)/\sigma_f]dt + dz_f$. Note that dz_f is not observable, whereas dz_f' is. The paths of μ_f^+ and z_f' therefore uniquely determine the path of dF/F. To see further that the path of μ_f^+ itself is generated by z_f', we can rewrite equation (6) as $d\mu_f^+ = -k\mu_f^+ dt + [(\rho\sigma_\mu\sigma_f + \sigma_e^+/\sigma_f]dz_f'$; the information structures generated by dz_f' and dF/F are therefore the same. However, as z_f' is a Brownian motion process, only the current values of F and μ_f^+ determine the probability distribution of F and μ_f^+ over the next interval. Further, the linear independence of dF/F on μ_f^+ makes μ_f^+ a state variable that appears in the utility function given by (13).

$$
\begin{aligned}
- J_t = \ & U(C/I,t) + J_y[E(dY)] \\
& + J_i\,[E(dI)] + J_\mu^+[E(d\mu_f^+)] + J_z[E(dZ)] \\
& + 1/2J_{yy}\mathrm{var}(dY) + 1/2J_{ii}\mathrm{var}(dI) \\
& + 1/2J_{\mu\mu}^+\mathrm{var}(d\mu_f^+) + 1/2J_{zz}\mathrm{var}(dZ) \\
& + J_{yi}\mathrm{cov}(dY,dI) + J_{y\mu}^+\mathrm{cov}(dY,d\mu_f^+) \\
& + J_{yz}\mathrm{cov}(dY,dZ) \\
& + J_{i\mu}^+\mathrm{cov}(dI,d\mu_f^+) \\
& + J_{\mu z}^+\mathrm{cov}(d\mu_f^+,dZ) + J_{iz}\mathrm{cov}(dI,dZ),
\end{aligned}
$$

(14)

where $E(dY)$ is the sum of all the terms in (12) that contain dt and other relevant terms are defined by:[10]

$$
\begin{aligned}
\mathrm{cov}(dY,dI) &= (w'W/I)V_{ai} &&+ (X'F/I)V_{fi} &&- (W/I^2)V_{ii} \\
\mathrm{cov}(dY,d\mu_f^+) &= (w'W/I)V_{a\mu}^+ &&+ (X'F/I)V_{f\mu}^+ &&- (W/I^2)V_{i\mu}^+ \\
\mathrm{cov}(dY,dz) &= (w'W/I)V_{az} &&+ (X'F/I)V_{fz} &&- (W/I^2)V_{iz} \\
\end{aligned}
$$

$$
\mathrm{var}(dY) = (w'W/I, X'F/I)
\begin{pmatrix} V_{aa} & V_{af} \\ V_{fa} & V_{ff} \end{pmatrix}
\begin{pmatrix} wW/I \\ XF/I \end{pmatrix}
- 2(W/I^2)\,(w'W/I, X'F/I)
\begin{pmatrix} V_{ai} \\ V_{fi} \end{pmatrix}.
$$

With these definitions in hand, the first-order conditions provide:

(15)
$$
\begin{pmatrix} 0 \\ 0 \end{pmatrix} = J_y
\begin{pmatrix} \mu_a - rl - V_{ai}/I \\ \mu_f^+ - V_{fi}/I \end{pmatrix}
+ J_{yy}
\begin{pmatrix} V_{aa} & V_{af} \\ V_{fa} & V_{ff} \end{pmatrix}
\begin{pmatrix} wW/I \\ XF/I \end{pmatrix}
$$
$$
- J_{yy}\begin{pmatrix} V_{ai} \\ V_{fi} \end{pmatrix}
+ J_{yi}\begin{pmatrix} V_{ai} \\ V_{fi} \end{pmatrix}
+ J_{y\mu}^+\begin{pmatrix} V_{a\mu}^+ \\ V_{f\mu}^+ \end{pmatrix}
+ J_{yz}\begin{pmatrix} V_{az} \\ V_{fz} \end{pmatrix}.
$$

To simplify (15), let us define the following quantities: $\theta = J_y/YJ_{yy}$ is the investor's coefficient of real relative risk tolerance; $w = (wW/I)/(W/I)$ is the portfolio weights of risky assets; the fraction $x = (XF/I)/(W/I)$ is the nominal \$U.S. value of foreign currency bought or sold for forward delivery taken as a proportion of current nominal wealth; $H_{yi} = J_{yi}/YJ_{yy}$ and $H_{y\mu}^+ = J_{y\mu}^+/YJ_{yy}$ are cross-preference coefficients; and the variance–covariance matrix is denoted by

10. Note that here V_{ff} is the *forecasted* variance of the vector dF/F. With $dF/F = \mu_f^+ dt + \sigma_f dz_f'$, we have $\mathrm{var}(dF/F) = \mathrm{var}(\mu_f^+ dt) + \mathrm{var}(\sigma_f dz_f')$. Instantaneously, $\mathrm{var}(\mu_f^+ dt) = 0$ as $\mu_f^+ dt$ is known and nonrandom. Notice that by virtue of (5), $\mathrm{var}(dz_f') = (1/\sigma_f^2)\,\mathrm{var}(e) + \mathrm{var}(dz_i)$, where $\mathrm{var}(e)$ is the unobservable true variance. We set $\mathrm{var}^+(e) = (\sigma_e^+)^2$, the estimated variance, so that $\mathrm{var}(dF/F) = \sigma_f'\sigma_f dt + (\sigma_e^+)^2 dt^2$, using notation from note 9 and the result that $dz_f'^2$ and dz_f^2 are of the order of dt. If, also, terms in dt^2 tend to 0, $V_{ff} = \sigma_f'\sigma_f$.

$$V = \begin{pmatrix} V_{aa} & V_{af} \\ V_{fa} & V_{ff} \end{pmatrix}.$$

These simplifications enable us to rewrite (15) as:

(16)
$$\begin{aligned}
\begin{pmatrix} w \\ x \end{pmatrix} = {} & \left[\theta V^{-1} \begin{pmatrix} \mu_a - rl \\ \mu_f^+ \end{pmatrix} \right. \\[4pt]
& \left. + (1-\theta) V^{-1} \begin{pmatrix} V_{ai}/I \\ V_{fi}/I \end{pmatrix} \right] \\[4pt]
& - \left[H_{yi} V^{-1} \begin{pmatrix} V_{ai} \\ V_{fi} \end{pmatrix} + H_{y\mu}^+ V^{-1} \begin{pmatrix} V_{a\mu}^+ \\ V_{f\mu}^+ \end{pmatrix} \right. \\[4pt]
& \left. + H_{yz} V^{-1} \begin{pmatrix} V_{az} \\ V_{fz} \end{pmatrix} \right].
\end{aligned}$$

The righthand side of (16) decomposes the investor's optimal demands into two major components. The top two rows together contain the efficient portfolio that, for a given risk tolerance, maximizes expected real return subject to a static variance constraint.[11] As written, it itself is the sum of two terms. The first, with weight θ, is the "log-portfolio," which is the one that is held by an investor whose utility function is logarithmic (the log-investor) and whose θ, therefore, is unity. The second is naturally identified as the minimum-variance portfolio (as it is the portfolio that unconditionally minimizes the variance of dY).[12] Any efficient portfolio can be constructed from linear combinations of these two. The log-portfolio will be a benchmark in what follows. Recall that the log-investor is both nationless and myopic: He maximizes expected nominal returns subject to a nominal variance constraint, without regard for inflation or

---

11. That is, it is the portfolio that up to a scalar multiple, $\lambda W/I = 1/\theta$, solves the program:

$$\max_{\{w,x\}} \; [\, w'(\mu_a - rl - V_{ai}/I) + x'(\mu_f^+ - V_{fi}/I) \,]$$

$$+ (\lambda/2) \{ k - (w'V_{aa}w + 2w'V_{af}x + x'V_{ff}x) \\
+ 2[(W/I^2)\,(w'V_{ai} + x'V_{fi})] \}$$

where k is a constant.

12. This is the portfolio that is held by an infinitely risk-averse investor whose $\theta = 0$. It solves the program:

$$\min_{\{w,x\}} \; [\, w'V_{aa}w + 2w'V_{af}x + x'V_{ff}x - 2(W/I)\,(w'V_{ai}/I + x'V_{fi}/I) \,]$$

any other state variable.[13] Alternatively, the log-portfolio is the only combination of risky assets that any investor will hold if inflation is nonstochastic and the efficient frontier is stationary.

The second component of the optimal asset demands consists of the Merton–Breeden hedge portfolios that we have collected in the bottom two rows of (16). These portfolios protect the investor against adverse shifts of the opportunity set, due to inflation, imperfect information and other state variables.[14]

We need a final transformation of (16) to bring out implications for hedging behavior beyond the introduction of state-variable hedges. We rewrite V^{-1} as:

$$(17) \quad \begin{pmatrix} V_{aa} & V_{af} \\ V_{fa} & V_{ff} \end{pmatrix}^{-1} = \begin{bmatrix} (V_{aa} - \beta' V_{ff}\beta)^{-1} & | & -(V_{aa} - \beta' V_{ff}\beta)^{-1}\beta' \\ & | & \\ -\beta(V_{aa} - \beta' V_{ff}\beta)^{-1} & | & V_{ff}^{-1} + \beta(V_{aa} - \beta' V_{ff}\beta)^{-1}\beta' \end{bmatrix}$$

where, following Sercu (1980), $\beta' = V_{af}V_{ff}^{-1}$ is the $(N \times L)$ matrix of the regression coefficients of the N assets on the L forward contracts; and $V_{aa} - \beta' V_{ff}\beta = V_{a \cdot f}$ is the $(N \times N)$ matrix of the residuals of these regressions. This is also the variance–covariance matrix of "hedged" asset returns, that is, of asset returns conditional on the forward exchange rate.

We substitute (17) into (16) and manipulate to get:

$$w = \theta V_{a \cdot f}^{-1}(\mu_a - rl - \beta'\mu_f^+) + (1 - \theta)V_{a \cdot f}^{-1}[(V_{ai}/I) - \beta'(V_{fi}/I)]$$

$$- H_{yi}V_{a \cdot f}^{-1}(V_{ai} - \beta' V_{fi}) - H_{y\mu}^+ V_{a \cdot f}^{-1}(V_{a\mu}^+ - \beta' V_{f\mu}^+)$$

$$(18) \qquad - H_{yz}V_{a \cdot f}^{-1}(V_{az} - \beta' V_{fz})$$

$$x = -\beta w + \theta V_{ff}^{-1}\mu_f^+ + (1 - \theta)V_{ff}^{-1}(V_{fi}/I)$$

$$- H_{yi}V_{ff}^{-1}V_{fi} - H_{y\mu}^+ V_{ff}^{-1}V_{f\mu}^+ - H_{yz}V_{ff}^{-1}V_{fz}.$$

The solution for w in (18) is a demand for risky assets that are hedged

---

13. See Adler and Detemple (1988) and the references therein. In the classic frictionless and unconstrained portfolio problem, the value function associated with logarithmic utility is additively separable between nominal wealth and inflation or state variables. The minimum-variance and all intertemporal hedging demands vanish.

14. These are the portfolios that solve the unconstrained program, $\max_{\{w,x\}} \text{cov}[dY, dJ_y(Y, I, \mu_f^+, Z)/J_{yy}]$, that maximizes the covariance between the change in real wealth and the relative change in the marginal utility of real wealth.

against exchange risk. Hedged risky assets are held as part of the efficient portfolio, to hedge against inflation, and to hedge the effects of imperfect information and of other state variables.

The demand for forward contracts has six components in (18), one of which is speculative. The last three, in the bottom row of the solution for x, are unambiguously intertemporal hedging demands in the sense of Merton and Breeden. The sum of the first three, in the top row, constitutes the demand for forward contracts as part of the instantaneously efficient portfolio. Within this sum, the third term, $(1-\theta)V_{fff}^{-1}(V_{fi}/I)$, represents (part of) the forward contracts that appear in the minimum-variance portfolio. As the purpose of minimizing variance is pure risk reduction, it is appropriate to classify this component as an inflation-hedge demand. It disappears and is replaced by the domestic riskless bond when inflation is deterministic and the efficient frontier is stationary.

This leaves the sum of the first two terms to represent the demand for forward contracts to be included in the log-portfolio. This log-portfolio demand has two parts. One, $-\beta w$, is for forward contracts to hedge the total of all (optimal) positions in risky assets: We label it the log-portfolio hedging demand. The other, $\theta V_{ff}^{-1}\mu_f^+$, can loosely be called the speculative component: It contains the speculative positions in each contract; it depends on the direction in which forward exchange rates are expected to move; and evidently it has nothing to do with reducing the risk of preestablished positions in the market portfolio, the usual definition of hedging.[15]

---

15. Defining $\theta V_{ff}^{-1}\mu_f^+$ in its entirety as the speculative component of the demand for forward contracts leaves in our minds something to be desired. One can further partition V_{ff} itself by separating the last, Lth, row and column. Inverting this partitioned V_{ff} matrix and postmultiplying by μ_f^+ produces $(L-1)$ hedged demands, for the other forward contracts, hedged by the Lth, plus a demand for the Lth. This last then contains a hedging component plus what irreducably and unambiguously is a speculative component, of the form $\theta\mu_{fl}^+/\sigma_{fl}^2$, where the subscript fl denotes the Lth forward contract. All this implies that the label speculative should in principle be restricted only to positions in each contract associated with its individual risk-preference-weighted Sharpe ratio: $\theta V_{ff}^{-1}\mu_f^+$ as a whole is then a speculative demand in the loose sense that it is the only portfolio that contains what are clearly speculative positions.

This discussion illustrates the semantic arbitrariness of attempts to distinguish speculation from hedging. There are those who identify speculation exclusively with position taking based on non-equilibrium or nonconsensus beliefs. This view precludes the possibility of speculation in homogeneous expectations models. All asset demands, by elimination, are then hedging demands. Others reserve hedging to describe only portfolios designed to reduce the impact of adverse fluctuations in the opportunity set due to the existence of nontraded assets and nontraded state variables. In this view, hedging cannot occur in stationary and frictionless markets with unlimited short selling: any hedging that appears to occur, as per equation (18), is arbitrarily the illusory byproduct of the efficient

To conclude this section we explore the implications of equation (18) for the ongoing debate as to whether foreign asset portfolios should be fully and permanently hedged against exchange risk. Perold and Schulman (1988) argue that they should be, based on certain stylized empirical facts: the long-run average (i.e., the unconditional) risk premium appears to be zero; and both the variance of the inflation rate and rollover transaction costs are small enough to ignore. In these circumstances, they argue, zero speculation and continuous hedging using unitary hedge ratios are optimal.

In contrast, equation (18) teaches us that several stringent conditions must be met for such a strategy to be optimal. Hedge ratios cannot be unitary unless (1) local-currency rates of return on risky assets are uncorrelated with dF/F; (2) inflation is either completely nonstochastic or uncorrelated with exchange rate changes; (3) other state variables either do not exist or are uncorrelated with forward contract returns; and (4) investors are never uncertain about the parameters of the risk premium process. In addition, it is the (estimated) conditional risk premium, not its long-run average, that must be continuously and identically equal to zero if the speculative demand is to disappear. All these conditions are violated empirically.

We should note at this point that by inference Black (1989) challenges Perold and Schulman from a different perspective. He claims to have discovered a universal hedge ratio which is the same for investors of all nations and is generally less than unity. We report on results from a companion paper, which subjects Black's result to a detailed analysis, in our fourth section.

III. BEHAVIORAL IMPLICATIONS OF IMPERFECT INFORMATION

This section seeks to explore how imperfect information about the forward risk premium affects the speculative and hedging components of

portfolio calculations.

Our taxonomy takes the middle ground. Any risk-averse investor chooses assets in simultaneous response to both speculative and hedging motives. The speculative motive generates those transactions that increase portfolio risk. The hedging motive produces all transactions that reduce overall portfolio risk. By this token, $\theta V_{ff}^{-1} \mu_f^+$ contains the speculative positions in each forward contract which, together, raise the log-portfolio's risk above the static, minimum-variance level after accounting for all intertemporal state-variable hedges.

an investor's demand for forward contracts. Our results show that the effect is indeterminate. Ambiguity arises from two sources. One is that uncertainty about forward risk premiums can change many elements of the estimated variance–covariance matrix in ways that are hard to measure without excessively strong simplifying assumptions. The other is that the direction of the state-variable hedge terms cannot in general be signed for most utility functions. These observations greatly limit what one is able to say about the way markets are likely to respond to changes in the availability of information.

Let us look at these issues more systematically. The consequence of introducing forecast errors in connection with forward risk premiums is twofold. First, their variances are increased next to the perfect information case and, in general, their covariances with all other risky assets and foreign currencies are changed. Second, each unobservable risk premium operates as a state variable whether or not it did so before. We know of only one case where the result is unambiguous. When his utility is logarithmic, the investor's $H_{y\mu}^+$ is zero, as are all the other state-variable hedges. One can also assume that uncertainty about forward risk premiums leaves all covariances and the demand for all other assets unchanged. It is then clear that imperfect information reduces the (speculative) demand for each forward contract. The neatness of this result disappears even in the logarithmic utility case, once covariances or other asset demands are allowed to change. When they do, log-portfolio weights that are positive under complete information can turn negative, and vice versa. The sign of the combined effect on the demand for any forward contract is ambiguous.

Allowing utility functions to be nonlogarithmic introduces problems of a different order. Referring to equations (13) and (14), the main issue for present purposes is this: can we identify a direct utility function, $U(C/I,t)$, for which the associated indirect or derived utility of wealth function, $J(Y,Z,\mu_f^+,t)$, is such that $J_{y\mu}^+$ has an unambiguous sign as $\mu_f^+ \gtrless 0$, i.e., given that the investor is long ($\mu_f^+ > 0$) or short the forward contract? This is what we need to know if we are to determine whether or not imperfect information causes investors to behave more cautiously or, in other words, whether the additional hedge term offsets the speculative term or reinforces it. The problem, unfortunately, is intractable. Like others before us, we have been unable to solve it.[16] As a consequence, $H_{y\mu}^+$ in equations (16) and (18) cannot be signed in general. This difficulty

16. It is known that when $U(C/I,t)$ belongs to the HARA class, $J(Y,Z,t) = F(Z,t)K(Y,t)$, where

in continuous time analysis calls into question the main static, one-period result of Klein and Bawa (1977).

To go as far as we can, we study the effective speculative demand for the ith forward contract defined from (18) as the sum of the speculative component of the demand for the ith currency and the intertemporal hedge against variations in its risk premium. In addition, we employ two properties of an investor's behavior when his information is imperfect: his forecasting precision and his forecasting performance.

Forecasting *precision* is defined, following equation (5), as $1/\text{var}^+(e_i)$, that is, as the reciprocal of the estimated variance of the unobservable forecasting error associated with the ith risk premium, denoted $1/\sigma_e^2$ for convenience. Complete information corresponds to $\sigma_e^2 = 0$ (infinite precision) in which case $\mu_f = \mu_f^+$.

In contrast, forecasting *power* can be measured only *ex post*. In equation (5) the investor forecasts μ_f. The true risk premium is not observable, however; only dF/F is. The best the investor can do is to predict μ_f^+ and to expect that dF/F will be distributed around it. These considerations suggest that, after the fact, a natural estimate of forecasting power can be obtained from the regression.[17]

$$(19) \qquad dF/F = a + b\mu_f^+ dt + \epsilon.$$

A significantly positive value of b indicates superior forecasting performance. Notice that $b = \text{cov}(dF/F, \mu_f^+ dt)/\text{var}(\mu_f^+ dt)$. *Ex post*, $\text{var}(\mu_f^+ dt)$ is what it is as a result of random changes in the forecast, $\mu_f^+ dt$, over time. Forecasting power is defined by the numerator of b and exists if $\text{cov}(dF/F, \mu_f^+ dt) > 0$. Clearly, the interval dt can no longer be infinitesimal

---

Z is any state variable affecting the opportunity set. The problem is to obtain an explicit solution for $F(Z,t)$ from the Bellman equation. Two approaches in the finance literature both had to assume only one risky asset in the economy. Merton (1971) assumed in addition a constant interest rate and CARA (exponential) utility. He was able to solve for J with a mean-reverting diffusion on the single risky asset. In this setting $(-J_{yz}/YJ_{yy})$ is independent of Z, with its sign depending on the parameters of the model. Ingersoll (1987, pp. 290–294) assumed a single asset (power utility), a stochastic interest rate which becomes a state variable, and a zero risk premium for the single risky asset. His result was that $(-J_{yz}/YJ_{yy}) \gtreqless 0$ as risk tolerance $\gtreqless$ unity, i.e., that of the logarithmic utility function. No further specialization is possible. Recently Karatzas assumed complete markets and showed the way to solve for $F(Z,t)$ explicitly in the presence of many assets and for general diffusion processes. However, the explicit solution for J_{yz} that is available in principle cannot, by reason of its complexity, be unambiguously signed.

17. This formulation of forecasting power is consistent with those of Henriksson and Merton (1981) and Cumby and Modest (1987).

if terms involving dt^2 are not to be ignored, as otherwise the coefficient b would be undefined.

There is a subtle link between forecasting power and precision. It is clear from equation (7) that the deterministic evolution of σ_e^2 forward from time t requires an initial value as its point of departure. This initial estimate can be obtained from an analysis of the variance of the error term in equation (19), which itself is estimated on data prior to time t. Note that $\sigma_e^2 dt^2 = \text{var}(\mu_f dt | \mu_f^+ dt)$ and that $\sigma_\epsilon^2 dt^2 = \text{var}(dF/F | \mu_f^+ dt) = \text{var}(\mu_f dt + \sigma_f dz_f | \mu_f^+ dt) = \text{var}(\mu_f dt | \mu_f^+ dt) + \text{var}(\sigma_f dz_f) = \sigma_e^2 dt^2 + \sigma_f^2 dt$. As we have assumed that σ_ϵ^2 and σ_f^2 are both known, the initial estimate of σ_e^2 can be extracted. The result that $\sigma_\epsilon^2 = \sigma_e^2 + (\sigma_f^2/dt)$ is intuitively pleasing. It tells us that greater precision in estimating μ_f^+ will improve the R^2 of equation (19) and raise one's confidence in his forecasting power by reducing $\text{var}(b) = \sigma_\epsilon^2/\text{var}(\mu_f^+ dt)$. Conversely, as σ_f^2 is known exogenously, a reduction in σ_ϵ^2 signals the investor that his precision has improved.

Finally, we define the effective speculative demand for the ith contract as the sum of the speculative and intertemporal hedging terms:

(20) $$q = \theta \mu_f^+ dt / v_f^2 - H_{y\mu}^+ (\sigma_{f\mu}^+ / v_f^2),$$

where:

$$v_f^2 = \text{var}(dF/F) = \text{var}(\mu_f^+ dt + \sigma_f dz_f')$$
from note 10; and
$$\sigma_{f\mu}^+ = \text{cov}(dF/F, d\mu_f^+).$$

We are now in a position to state the two propositions that are the main contribution of this section.

Proposition 1: Forecasting Power (FP)

An increase (decrease) in forecasting power $[FP = \text{cov}(dF/F, \mu_f^+ dt)]$ after time 0: (i) leaves the speculative demand unaffected and (ii) reduces (raises) the absolute value of the hedging demand. The effective speculative demand increases (decreases) depending on the sign of $H_{y\mu}^+$.

Proof: Part (i) of the proposition is immediate: The speculative term depends by definition on the predicted μ_f^+ but not on the ability to forecast it. Since σ_e^+ is deterministic after time 0, changes in FP cannot affect it or, therefore, $\text{var}(dF/F.)$ The initial estimate of μ_f^+, which determines the initial speculative demand, also depends on past FP. Changes in FP

after time 0 consequently leave the speculative demand intact. Part (ii) follows directly from the fact that we can write $\sigma_{f\mu}^{+}$ out fully as:[18]

□ $\sigma_{\mu f}^{+} = (\rho\sigma_{\mu}\sigma_{f} + \sigma_{e}^{2})[1 + (\sigma_{e}^{2}/\sigma_{f}^{2})]dt - [k + (1/\sigma_{f}^{2})(\rho\sigma_{\mu}\sigma_{f} + \sigma_{e}^{2})](FP).$

Proposition 2: Forecasting Precision

For a given risk premium forecast, μ_{f}^{+}, a rise (fall) in forecasting precision ($\equiv 1/\sigma_{e}^{2}$): increases (reduces) the speculative demand unambiguously and reduces (raises) the absolute value of the hedging demand. The net effect depends on the sign of $H_{y\mu}^{+}$.

Proof:[19] By differentiating $\delta q/\delta\sigma_{e}^{2}$.

We conclude this section by drawing attention to the similarities and differences between the Kalman–Bucy (K-B) filter embodied in equation

---

18. Recall equation (6). The covariance in the numerator of the hedging demand can be written as:

$$\sigma_{f\mu}^{+} = -k\,\text{cov}(dF/F, u_{f}^{+}\,dt) + (1/\sigma_{f}^{2})\,(\rho\sigma_{\mu}\sigma_{f} + \sigma_{e}^{2})\,[\text{cov}(dF/F, dF/F)$$
$$- \text{cov}(dF/F, \mu_{f}^{+}\,dt)]$$

where

$$\text{cov}(dF/F, dF/F) = \text{var}(dF/F) = \sigma_{f}^{2}dt + \sigma_{e}^{2}dt^{2}.$$

Hence:

$$\sigma_{f\mu}^{+} = (\rho\sigma_{\mu}\sigma_{f} + \sigma_{e}^{2})\,[1 + (\sigma_{e}^{2}/\sigma_{f}^{2})]dt$$
$$- [k + (1/\sigma_{f}^{2})\,(\rho\sigma_{\mu}\sigma_{f} + \sigma_{e}^{2})]\text{cov}(dF/F, \mu_{f}^{+}\,dt),$$

which is the form in the text.

19. All parts of this proof require the definition of the denominator: $v^{2} = \text{var}(dF/F) = \text{var}(\mu_{f}^{+}\,dt + \sigma_{f}dz_{f}') = \sigma_{f}^{2}\text{var}(dz_{f}')$, given that $\text{var}(\mu_{f}^{+}\,dt) = 0$ as $\mu_{f}^{+}\,dt$ is nonrandom. Following note 10, we replace the unobservable variance of the true error in $\text{var}(dz_{f}')$ with its estimate, so that $\sigma_{f}^{2}\text{var}(dz_{f}') = \sigma_{f}^{2}dt + \sigma_{e}^{2}dt^{2}$. Now, differentiate the speculative term:

$$\partial(\theta\mu_{f}^{+}/v^{2})/\partial\sigma_{e}^{2} = -\theta\mu_{f}^{+}dt/v^{4} \gtreqless 0 \text{ as } \mu_{f}^{+} \gtreqless 0.$$

To analyze the hedging term, we combine $dF/F = \mu_{f}^{+}\,dt + \sigma_{f}dz_{f}'$ with equation (6), rewritten as $d\mu_{f}^{+} = -k\mu_{f}^{+}\,dt + A(dF/F - \mu_{f}^{+}\,dt)$, where $A = (\rho\sigma_{\mu}\sigma_{f} + \sigma_{e}^{2})/\sigma_{f}^{2}$. Substituting for dF/F, we obtain $d\mu_{f}^{+} = -k\mu_{f}^{+}\,dt + A\sigma_{f}dz_{f}'$. Hence, $\text{cov}(dF/F, d\mu_{f}^{+})$ is given by

$$\sigma_{f\mu}^{+} = -k\text{var}(\mu_{f}^{+}\,dt) + \sigma_{f}(A - k)\text{cov}(\mu_{f}^{+}\,dt, dz_{f}') + A\sigma_{f}^{2}\text{var}(dz_{f}') = A\sigma_{f}^{2}\text{var}(dz_{f}'),$$

as $\text{var}(\mu_{f}^{+}\,dt) = 0 = \text{cov}(\mu_{f}^{+}\,dt, dz_{f}')$ since $\mu_{f}^{+}\,dt$ is known. With this expression in hand, we can write the hedging term as

$$-H_{y\mu}^{+}[A\sigma_{f}^{2}\text{var}(dz_{f}')]/[\sigma_{f}^{2}\text{var}(dz_{f}')] = -H_{y\mu}^{+}A.$$

Differentiating, $\partial(-H_{y\mu}^{+}A)/\partial\sigma_{e}^{2} = -H_{y\mu}^{+}/\sigma_{f}^{2}$ by the definition of A.

(6) and technical trading rules. Following note 19, equation (6) can be written as $d\mu_f^+ = -k\mu_f^+ dt + A(dF/F - \mu_f^+ dt)$. Since $\mu_{ft+1}^+ = \mu_{ft}^+ + d\mu_f^+$, where $(t+1) - t = dt$, we have:

$$(21) \qquad \mu_{ft+1}^+ = (1-k)\mu_{ft}^+ dt + A_t(dF/F_t - \mu_{ft}^+ dt),$$

where A_t is the K-B filter parameter, $(\rho\sigma_\mu\sigma_f + \sigma_e^2)/\sigma_f^2$, and the second term in (21) is the process whereby one updates his estimate of the risk premium. Solving (21) recursively produces:

$$(22) \qquad \mu_{f_{n+1}}^+ = A_n(\frac{dF}{F})_n + \{\sum_{i=0}^{n-1} A_i(\frac{dF}{F})_i [\prod_{j=i+1}^{n} (1-k-A_j)]\}$$
$$+ \prod_{i=0}^{n}(1-k-A_i)\mu_{f_0}^+.$$

Equation (22) shows that the current forecast of the risk premium is given by a (moving) average of past price changes provided only that the initial forecast, $\mu_{f_0}^+$, itself is based on past prices. This establishes the similarity of the K-B filter to a TTR, though not one that is described in the 1981 Technical Commodity Yearbook.

There are differences, of course. Garden-variety TTRs are pure trend-following devices that have no objective that they optimize, whereas our K-B rule minimizes forecast variance. TTRs that signal the direction of trading leave its magnitude unspecified, whereas the latter is governed in the K-B rule by the size of the speculative position in equation (20). Following a buy or sell signal, most TTRs are characterized by periods of inactivity for as long as trends last, whereas the K-B filter will tend to modify the size of the position whenever $dF/F \neq \mu_f^+ dt$. It is even impossible to say whether, whenever TTRs produce profits, the K-B filter does also.

These differences notwithstanding, the point remains: Markets with imperfectly informed traders will reveal what appears to be technical trading behavior. This is an innovation compared to the position-taking rules inherent in static perfect-information models. An outstanding issue is how frequently the initial risk premium estimate, $\mu_{f_0}^+$, itself should be revised.

IV. ON THE POSSIBILITY OF UNIVERSAL HEDGE RATIOS

This section summarizes results from a companion paper (Adler and Prasad, 1989). The issue is whether there is a way of stating a hedging policy that is invariant across investors and is the same for all, regardless of nationality. Could such a policy be specified, it would greatly simplify the design of currency hedges for international portfolios. Here we investigate the conditions for the existence of such policies. The outcome of this study is twofold. First, when nationalities are distinguished by investors' consumption mixes and utility functions, no universal hedge ratio (UHR) exists when inflation is stochastic or when imperfect information and/or other state variables randomize the opportunity set. Second, any possibility of a UHR is then necessarily restricted to a world with nonstochastic price levels and stationary efficient frontiers. Although UHRs can be defined in various ways in this arid setting, all are associated exclusively with the weights of foreign and domestic bonds within what we called in Section I the log-portfolio. As soon as the investor's variance-reducing hedge portfolios include more than just the domestic bond, no UHR is available.

To develop these points, let us proceed from the simplest situation based on the assumptions of Solnik (1974). We assume everywhere complete information, deterministic inflation rates, and stationary opportunity frontiers. In this case, each investor holds a combination of the log-portfolio and his domestic default-free bond. As the domestic bond is riskless, it no longer features in the set of risky assets and must be accounted for separately. For investor u, the asset demands of equation (18) then appear as follows:

$$w^u = \theta^u [V_{a \cdot f}^{-1} (\mu_a - rl - \beta' \mu_f)]^u$$

(23) $$x^u = -\beta^u w^u + \theta^u (V_{ff}^{-1} \mu_f)^u$$

$$x_u^u = [\theta^u (1 - l'w^u) - 1'x^u] + (1 - \theta^u).$$

In (23), w^u is the vector of equity weights in the log-portfolio, $[V_{a \cdot f}^{-1}(\mu_a - rl - \beta'\mu_f)]$, as priced in currency u. Previously, x^u denoted a vector of forward contracts, whereas here x^u represents equally correctly the vector of foreign bond weights; as these are risky, all are held only in the log-portfolio. There are two components of the demand, x_u^u, for the domestic riskless bond. The first, its weight in the log-portfolio, is determined as a residual; the second, $(1 - \theta^u)$, is the fraction of investor u's wealth that he holds in the domestic bond outside the log-portfolio.

The source of all possible invariance results is the fact, explicitly demonstrated by Sercu (1980), that every log-portfolio weight, including those of domestic and foreign bonds, remains constant under a change of numeraire (i.e., measurement currency). These weights are therefore equal for all investors, regardless of nationality, even though the bond that is deemed domestic changes as one shifts perspective. However, no position held outside the log-portfolio remains similarly unchanged unless investors' wealth endowments and risk tolerances are identical.

Owing to these considerations, it is natural to focus the search for UHRs on one or other of the characteristics of the demands for bonds inside the log-portfolio. Once bonds outside the log-portfolio are included in the definition of a hedge, no UHR can be found. Given this restriction, two kinds of UHR can be identified. The first, espoused by Black (1989), identifies the UHR with the sum of all bonds, domestic and foreign, within the log-portfolio. The second, our contribution, associates the UHR with what in Section II we called the hedging components of the demands for foreign bonds. Let us examine each in turn.

Proposition 3: UHR(1) (Black, 1989)

The sum of the weights of all bonds in the log-portfolio is equal for every investor. This sum is a possible UHR and is given by $\theta^m - 1$, where θ^m is the market risk tolerance.

That the *sum* of the bond weights in the log-portfolio is equal for every investor follows trivially from the fact that *each* weight is equal across investors. Black could have stopped here. His main insight does not require aggregation. Following Adler and Dumas (1983, corollary 2), we now show that this sum, appropriately scaled, is $\theta^m - 1$. To this end we assume that each bond is in zero net supply. Multiply both sides of each of the demand equations in (23) by W^u, investor u's current wealth; following Sercu, drop the superscript on the log-portfolio; next, sum separately his stock investments (across risky assets) and his investments in foreign bonds; and omit the domestic bond position outside the log-portfolio:

$$
\begin{aligned}
&\text{(i) } l'w^u W^u & &= \theta^u w^u [\, l' V_{a \cdot f}^{-1} (\mu_a - rl - \beta' \mu_f)\,] \\
\text{(24)} \quad &\text{(ii) } l'x^u W^u & &= -l'\beta^u W^u + \theta^u (l' V_{ff}^{-1} \mu_f) \\
&\text{(iii) } x_{u,\log}^u W^u & &= \theta^u W^u (1 - l'w^u) - l'x W^u.
\end{aligned}
$$

The ratio we seek is (investor u's holdings of all bonds in the log-portfolio) divided by (investor u's investment in the world market portfolio). The numerator is obtained by adding 24(ii) and 24(iii), which gives $\theta^u W^u (1 - \beta' w^u)$; the denominator is the RHS of 24(i). Substituting and dividing,

(25) $\text{UHR}(1) = [1 - l'V_{a \cdot f}^{-1}(\mu_a - rl - \beta'\mu_f)]/[l'V_{a \cdot f}^{-1}(\mu_a - rl - \beta'\mu_f)].$

As the stock component of the log-portfolio, $l'V_{a \cdot f}^{-1}(\mu_a - rl - \beta'\mu_f)$, is the same for everyone, this UHR is independent of the investor's nationality. This could be the end of the story. To simplify (25) further, aggregate 24(i) across investors. Note than when the aggregate supply of each bond is zero, $\Sigma_u \, l'w^u W^u = \Sigma_u W^u = \text{total world wealth}$. Hence,

(26) $\Sigma_u W^u = \Sigma_u \theta^u W^u [l'V_{a \cdot f}^{-1}(\mu_a - rl - \beta'\mu_f)],$

Define $\theta^m = (\Sigma_u \theta^u W^u)/\Sigma_u W^u$ as the world market risk tolerance. Equation (26) then produces

(27) $1/\theta^m = l'V_{a \cdot f}^{-1}(\mu_a - rl - \beta'\mu_f),$

and equation (25) reduces to

(28) $\text{UHR}(1) = [1 - (1/\theta^m)]/(1/\theta^m) = \theta^m - 1.$

The additive inverse of (28), $1 - \theta^m$, is Black's "equilibrium hedge" ratio.[20] His definition is highly problematic for a number of reasons.

First, a hedge ratio based on the sum of all bonds in the log-portfolio leaves unspecified what one most needs to know in practice: how much of each bond to buy or sell. One cannot even determine the total of all bonds to be bought or sold because each investor's position in his domestic bond *outside* the log-portfolio has been left out. As soon as it is admitted, the possibility of a UHR disappears. The sum of all bond positions inside and outside the log-portfolio, per unit holding of the market portfolio, generally differs across investors.[21]

20. Black labeled the investor's domestic bond position outside the log-portfolio, $(1 - \theta^u)W^u$, as his "gross domestic lending" and his total position in all bonds, foreign and domestic, inside the log-portfolio as his "gross borrowing." Since each bond is in zero net supply, (gross domestic lending) = $-$ (gross borrowing). He then (implicitly) defined his UHR to be world gross lending as a fraction of world wealth. Summing across investors,

$$\Sigma_u(1 - \theta^u)W^u W^m = (\Sigma_u W^u/W^m) - (\Sigma_u \theta^u W^u/W^m) = 1 - \theta^m.$$

21. The proof is trivial. All one needs is to add $(1 - \theta^u)W^u$, the domestic bond position for investor u, to 24(ii) and thereby to the numerator of (25). The resulting ratio of the investor's total investment in all bonds to his investment in the market portfolio is no longer independent of nationality. This ratio can be equal across investors if nations disappear, that is, if investors' endowments and utility functions are identical.

Second, when one sums 24(ii) and 24(iii) to obtain the numerator of (25), each investor's total position in bonds foreign to him cancels out. For any given investor, the counterintuitive result is that his foreign currency hedge consists purely of a position in his domestic bond. Surely, if one wants to remove currency risk from his holdings of the market portfolio, he expects to use foreign bonds for that purpose.

Third, Black's approach elides the possibly semantic distinction between the speculative and the hedging components of the demands for forward contracts. This is unfortunate, as the existence of forward risk premiums in this kind of partial pure exchange equilibrium is usually seen to depend on the presence of both speculative and hedging transactions.

Other problems arise in connection with Black's attempt to measure θ''' as a simple observable ratio involving only the mean market excess rate of return and the variances, respectively, of the market portfolio and exchange rates. The simplification comes at the cost of inconsistently having to define market aggregates using nonmarket weights. The details need not concern us here. The more important question is the development of more appealing alternatives to his definition of a hedge.

An intuitively acceptable definition of a hedge has two characteristics: (1) It corresponds to a position in foreign bonds and (2) it quantifies the amount of each foreign bond to hold, whether for hedging or for speculative purposes or both together. There are but two statements of UHRs that meet these requirements. Both, to repeat, are also restricted to the setting in which investors choose only combinations of the log-portfolio and their domestic bond.

Proposition 4: UHR(2)

The total (i.e., speculative plus hedging) demand for any given bond, per unit holding of the market portfolio, will be the same for all investors for whom that bond is foreign.

For any investor, foreign bonds are held only in the log-portfolio. Proposition 4 therefore follows directly from the fact that the log-portfolio weights for all bonds are equal across investors. As a practical prescription, however, UHR(2) is open to several of the criticisms leveled against UHR(1).

The demand for any foreign bond or forward contract can be decomposed, following the procedures of Section 1, into hedging and speculative components. The next proposition is less intuitive.

Proposition 5: UHR(3)

The hedging component of the demand for any given bond, per unit holding of the market portfolio (i.e., its beta with the market portfolio, β_i^k) will be the same for all investors from whose perspective that bond is foreign:

$$\beta_i^k = \beta_i^j, \ \forall \ i \neq j,k.$$

The nontrivial proof can be supplied on request. It reveals an additional relationship. In a two-country world, $\beta_1^2 + \beta_2^1 = 1$, where β_i^j is the beta of the market portfolio on the ith bond from the perspective of currency j. In an n-country world the relationship generalizes to

$$(29) \qquad\qquad \sum_{i \neq j} \beta_i^j = 1 - \beta_j^k \ \forall \ k \neq j.$$

What this says is that the sum of the beta hedge ratios for all foreign bonds with the market portfolio for any investor, say j, plus the beta of his bond measured from the perspective of any other investor, k, is unity. The U.S. investor regresses the market portfolio valued in \$U.S. on the set of currencies foreign to him. The German and Japanese do likewise with the market portfolio valued in their respective currencies. The sum of the betas in the U.S. investor's regression is then equal to unity minus the coefficient of the \$U.S. bond in either the German or the Japanese regression, these last two being equal by proposition 4. This is a technical result that depends only on the characteristics of the log-portfolio and not at all on aggregation or conditions for equilibrium.

We emphasize at this point that disappointingly, no UHR can be identified once bonds outside the log-portfolio are included in the hedge portfolio. Neither part of proposition 3 survives, as we have seen, when the sum of all bonds is taken to include, also, each investor's position in his domestic bond outside the log-portfolio. Finally, everything breaks down when, for any reason, foreign bonds are held outside the log-portfolio. This is easiest to see if we relax only the assumption of deterministic inflation (but continue to exclude all state variables, including inflation). Equation (18) in this slightly extended setting then becomes:

$$(30) \quad w^u = \theta^u[V_{a\cdot f}^{-1}(\mu_a - rl - \beta'\mu_f)] + (1 - \theta^u)V_{a\cdot f}^{-1}[(V_{ai}^u/I^u) - \beta'(V_{fi}^u/I^u)]$$

$$x^u = -\beta^u w^u + \theta^u(V_{ff}^{-1}\mu_f) + (1 - \theta^u)V_{ff}^{-1}(V_{fi}^u/I^u),$$

where x^u now includes the domestic bond, which is risky in real terms. Clearly, each investor now holds a portfolio containing stocks and foreign and domestic bonds in a minimum-variance hedge portfolio whose composition depends on the investor's idiosyncratic inflation rate. To continue to define hedging exclusively in connection with log-portfolio positions is, on the face of it, no longer reasonable. But as soon as one admits the hedge-portfolio demands, the possibility of a UHR of any kind obviously disappears. The presence of any state-variable hedge portfolio has exactly the same implication. In particular, imperfect information renders the concept of a UHR vacuous: Even were all investors' information equally imperfect, their hedge ratios would generally differ unless they were otherwise identical.

V. CONCLUSIONS

In finance, more information need not mean better information. The globalization of improved accounting standards is likely to provide investors with more information. Whether the increment will constitute better information that tightens their forecasting precision and improves their forecasting performance is debatable. Finance models tell us nothing about how investors or markets will react to more comprehensive data regarding the past. The bad news in this paper is that completely specified intertemporal asset demand models cannot tell us unambiguously how individuals or market equilibriums will respond to better information that is publicly and universally available. We therefore consider forecasts of international capital flows or world stock market behavior based on foreseeable changes in corporate financial reporting standards in the 1990s to be highly hazardous.

This said, two points remain to be made. The globalization of information is desirable on social grounds to the extent that it removes informational asymmetries. There is an evolving consensus that level playing fields in the international capital markets are preferable to the alternative. Second, improved and uniform worldwide financial reporting standards do more than serve the objective of informational symmetry. They also contribute to the precision of equity analysis and, more importantly, to the ability of owners to monitor managers. In a world with agency and contracting costs, reducing monitoring expense is likely to be found to be unambiguously good.

REFERENCES

Adler, M., and J. B. Detemple. 1988. "On the Optimal Hedge of a Nontraded Cash Position." *Journal of Finance* 43, no. 1 (March), 143–153.

Adler, M., and B. Dumas. 1983. "International Portfolio Choice and Corporation Finance: A Synthesis." *Journal of Finance* 38, no. 3 (June), 925–984.

Adler, M., and B. Prasad. 1989. "On Universal Currency Hedges." Columbia University Working Paper (October).

Black, F. 1989. "Equilibrium Exchange Rate Hedging." *N.B.E.R.* Working Paper, No. 2947 (April).

Breeden, D. T. 1984. "Futures Markets and Commodity Options: Hedging and Optimality in Incomplete Markets." *Journal of Economic Theory* 32 (April), 275–300.

Cox, J. C., Ingersoll, J. E., and S. A. Ross. 1985. "A Theory of the Term Structure of Interest Rates." *Econometrica* 53 (March), 363–383.

Cumby, R. F., and D. M. Modest. 1987. "Testing for Market Timing Ability: A Framework for Forecast Evaluation." *Journal of Financial Economics* 19, no. 1 (September), 169–189.

Detemple, J. B. 1986. "Asset Pricing in a Production Economy with Incomplete Information." *Journal of Finance* 41, no. 2 (June), 383–391.

Domowitz, I., and C. S. Hakkio. 1985. "Conditional Variance and the Risk Premium in the Foreign Exchange Market." *Journal of International Economics* 19, no. 1/2 (August), 47–66.

Dothan, U., and D. Feldman. 1986. "Equilibrium Interest Rates and Multiperiod Bonds in a Partially Observable Economy." *Journal of Finance* 41, no. 2 (June), 369–382.

Fama, E. F. 1984. "Forward and Spot Exchange Rates." *Journal of Monetary Economics* 14 (November), 319–338.

Gennotte, G. 1986. "Optimal Portfolio Choice under Incomplete Information." *Journal of Finance* 41 (July, Papers and Proceedings), 733–746.

Giovannini, A., and P. Jorion. 1987. "Interest Rates and Risk Premia in the Stock Market and in the Foreign Exchange Market." *Journal of International Money and Finance* 6 (March), 107–123.

Giovannini, A., and P. Jorion. 1989. "The Time-Variation of Risk and Return in the Foreign Exchange and Stock Markets." *Journal of Finance* 44, no. 2 (June), 307–325.

Henriksson, R. D., and R. C. Merton. 1981. "On Market Timing and Investment Performance, II: Statistical Procedures for Evaluating Forecasting Skills." *Journal of Business* 54, no. 4 (October), 513–533.

Ingersoll, J. E. 1987. *Theory of Financial Decision Making*. Totowa, NJ: Rowman and Littlefield.

Karatzas, I. Forthcoming. "Optimization Problems in the Theory of Continuous Trading." *SIAM Journal on Control and Optimization*.

Klein, R. W., and V. S. Bawa. 1977. "The Effect of Limited Information and Estimation Risk on Optimal Portfolio Diversification." *Journal of Financial Economics* 5, no. 1 (August), 89–111.

Lipster, R. S., and A. N. Shiryayev. 1977. *Statistics of Random Processes I and II*. New York: Springer-Verlag.

Merton, R. C. 1971. "Optimum Consumption and Portfolio Rules in a Continuous Time Model." *Journal of Economic Theory* 3, no. 4 (December), 373–413.

Merton, R. C. 1973. "An Intertemporal Capital Asset Pricing Model." *Econometrica* 41 (September), 867–887.

Perold, A. F., and E. C. Schulman. 1988. "The Free-Lunch in Hedging: Implications for Investment

Policy and Performance Standards.'' *Financial Analysts Journal* 44, no. 3 (May–June), 45–50.

Sercu, P. 1980. ''A Generalization of the International Asset Pricing Model.'' *Finance: Revue de l'Association Française de Finance* 1, no. 1 (June), 91–135.

Solnik, B. H. 1974. ''An Equilibrium Model of the International Capital Market.'' *Journal of Economic Theory* 8 (August), 500–524.

Wolff, C.C.P. 1984. ''Forward Foreign Exchange Rates, Expected Spot Rates and Premia: A Signal-Extraction Approach.'' *Journal of Finance* 42, no. 2 (June), 395–406.

Comments

EDWIN J. ELTON*

Over the past twenty years there has been a multitude of studies that demonstrate that international diversification should improve the investment performance of investors in all countries. The basic argument is a risk argument. The risk on a large, well-diversified domestic portfolio is almost completely market related. For U.S. mutual funds, about 95 percent of total risk is determined by aggregate movement in the U.S. equity market. International markets are relatively uncorrelated. Even though unhedged foreign markets are generally more risky than domestic, the low correlation implies that a combination of a domestic portfolio and an unhedged foreign portfolio is less risky than the domestic alone. Because of the reduction in risk, even if foreign markets return less than domestic, international diversification pays.

The unresolved issue in international investment is the amount and effect of foreign currency hedging. The effect of foreign currency hedging is a major current research topic with papers by Black (2), Perold and Schulman (4), and Kaplinis and Schaefer (3) all examining the issue. The paper by Adler and Prasad (1) is part of this literature. Empirically, most authors have shown that foreign currency hedging lowers the risk of the portfolio. Foreign currency hedging reduces the risk of foreign investment by eliminating the effect of currency fluctuations and thereby reducing the variance of return on foreign investment. Empirically, the effect of currency hedging on the correlation between domestic and foreign portfolios is relatively neutral. However, foreign currency hedging can impact expected returns, and therefore the net effect on portfolio performance is of interest.

The strength of the Adler and Prasad approach is its generality. They argue that empirical evidence supports the proposition that the risk premium on foreign currency in the long run converges to zero but in short periods is mean reverting and correlated. This is explicitly modeled, as are asset-returns, inflation and an optimum forecasting model of the mean risk premium. This allows the authors to examine very precisely the

*Stern Graduate School of Business, New York University.

conditions under which the more restrictive models of other authors hold. This is very useful in evaluating when these models might be reasonable approximations. Adler and Prasad do extensive analysis concerning how changes in some parameters might impact the amount that is hedged.

Clearly, hedging is the most important issue in international diversification. The Adler–Prasad paper provides a very general and useful analysis of this issue.

REFERENCES

Adler, M., and B. Prasad. 1989. "On Universal Currency Hedges." Columbia University Working Paper (October).

Black, F. 1989. "Equilibrium Exchange Rate Hedging." *N.B.E.R.* Working Paper, No. 2947 (April).

Kaplinis and Schaefer. "Exchange Risk and International Diversification in Bond and Equity Portfolios." Unpublished manuscript (1989). London Business School.

Perold, A. F., and E. C. Schulman. 1988. "The Free-Lunch in Hedging: Implications for Investment Policy and Performance Standards." *Financial Analysts Journal* 44, no. 3 (May–June), 45–50.

Trading/Nontrading Time Effect in French Futures Markets

Helyette Geman,* Uttama Savanayana,** and
Thomas Schneeweis**

I. INTRODUCTION

A growing body of academic literature has examined trading/nontrading time effect on the risk and return characteristics of various securities in U.S. financial markets. Trading time refers to the period in which a security is openly traded in either a central market (e.g., NYSE, CBOT) or an active over-the-counter market. Nontrading time covers those periods in which the principal market where a security is traded is closed. For the United States, trading/nontrading time effect studies have been conducted in the cash [13] as well as the futures markets [9, 17]. Most of these studies [9, 13, 17] have focused on differing returns/variances between weekdays and weekends.[1] Recent studies [21, 28] have also tested for intertemporal changes in asset risk as measured by return variance of overnight and daytime periods as well as intraday time intervals. Results in both the cash [21] and the futures markets [17, 28] indicate greater return variance during trading time than during nontrading time.

Although extensive analysis has taken place on the trading and nontrading time effect for the U.S. futures and cash markets, little research exists for the return/risk distribution patterns for securities in other countries. Empirical studies, which have focused only on the trading/nontrading periods in the U.S. markets, have failed to address the question of trading/nontrading effect on the pattern of returns and risk in other countries. Likewise, tests [17, 12] on the impact of macroinformation releases in the United States on asset prices fail to consider the effect of

*ESSEC, Cergy-Pontoise, France.
**School of Management, University of Massachusetts, Amherst.

1. Some studies ([17], [36]) have also reported a consistent negative price movement over weekends. Phillips-Patrick and Schneeweis [45], however, have shown that the weekend effect for cash and futures markets may be due in part to how security return is measured (e.g., inclusive of dividend and interest rate effects).

similar releases in foreign countries. Due to differing market structures, trading operations, and information flows in foreign security markets, the patterns of risk estimates across trading and nontrading periods as well as the reaction to macroeconomic information releases in foreign markets can differ substantially from those observed in U.S. markets.

In this paper we analyze the trading/nontrading time effect in the distribution of variance for the French Notionelle futures contract traded on the French MATIF. In addition, we test for the impact of macroinformation release dates (e.g., French money supply) on trading and nontrading time variances. Previous studies [21, 26] have suggested that measured risk (e.g., variance) is primarily a function of the likelihood of the arrival of unexpected information and the relative transaction costs of acting on the information. In the next section, we review alternative theories for the trading/nontrading time effect as well as the impact of information arrival process on the nonstationarity of return variance. Empirical results of tests on trading/nontrading time and information effects on return variance in U.S. and foreign markets are also briefly discussed. In Section III, the structure of the MATIF and the data and methodology for this analysis are presented. The distribution of variances of price changes for the French Notionelle futures contract is analyzed for the period November 17, 1986, to April 27, 1989. This period is also broken into three 200-day subperiods.[2] In order to concentrate on the impact of specific public macroeconomic information releases, days on which French money supply and trade balance figures are released are analyzed separately. Finally, since the period of analysis includes the October 1987 crash, the impact of the crash on reported results is also presented. The results of the analysis of the distribution of variances over the trading and nontrading periods for the French Notionelle futures contract is presented in Section IV. A summary and a discussion of the implications of information generated in international markets and differences in market structures for research on nonstationarity of asset return variance are presented in Section V.

The results of this study show that for the period of time examined, the reported variances of price changes differ between trading and nontrading hours of the French Notionelle futures contract.[3] In contrast to

2. The three subperiods are (1) November 17, 1986, to September 4, 1987, (2) September 5, 1987, to June 22, 1988, and (3) June 23, 1987, to April 27, 1989.

3. In this paper, variances were obtained using opening and closing prices. Analysis was also conducted on the variance of trading time using high and low prices (see [44]). Results were similar

results for U.S. security markets, the variances of the French Notionelle futures contract were often greater during nontrading than trading periods. However, for the days of French public macroinformation release (money supply and trade balance figures), the variances of price changes over trading and nontrading periods were relatively similar. These results tend to confirm a global information and transaction cost explanation for the differentials in variances reported between markets; that is, if the U.S. dollar is the principal currency for international transactions, then changes in information that affect U.S. dollar and interest rates may produce an impact on French opening prices that is greater than the impact of information released during the French futures market trading day on closing French futures prices. However, on those days when macroinformation is released that affects primarily the domestic market, price reaction is captured in the domestic French market and trading and nontrading time variances are more similar.

II. TRADING/NONTRADING EFFECT, INFORMATION IMPACT, AND NONSTATIONARITY OF ASSET RISK

Evidence of nonstationarity of asset risk as measured by return variance has been documented in several studies for both cash and futures markets. This nonstationarity in asset return variance has often been discussed in the context of calendar time and trading time (transaction time) hypotheses. Calendar time hypothesis posits that the stationary asset return–generating process operates continuously in calendar time with independent and identically distributed returns. If variances are generated according to the calendar time hypothesis, then variance over varying calendar time periods should be simple multiples of one another (e.g., the variance of a three-day weekend, Friday-close to Monday-close, should be three times the variance of any single calendar day, for example Tuesday-close to Wednesday-close). In contrast to the calendar time hypothesis, the trading time hypothesis maintains that the return-generating process operates continuously during trading time only. If the trading time hypothesis is correct, variance measured over a weekend, which includes one trading interval (Monday-open to Monday-close), should be

to those reported in this paper. Tests were also conducted using data on the MATIF contracts obtained from alternative sources (e.g., MATIF). The results were similar to those reported in this paper.

equal to variance on other weekdays, which also contains one trading period (Wednesday-open to Wednesday-close). Results of most studies, however, offer no conclusive support for either hypothesis (e.g., Fama [19], Oldfield and Rogalski [43]).

Several studies have also reported evidence of nonstationarity of variance across trading and nontrading time periods; that is, the return variance appears to be significantly greater over trading than nontrading hours of the markets (e.g., Cornell [13]; Dyl and Maberly [17]; French and Roll [21]; and Hill, Schneeweis, and Yau [28]). Various hypotheses including market structure (Goldman and Sosin [24]; Marsh and Webb [40]) and information impact (French and Roll [21]; Jordan, Seale, Dinehart, and Kenyon [33]) have been advanced as explanations for the trading/nontrading time effect in return variance patterns. The information explanation for variance differential over trading and nontrading periods is that asset return volatility changes in response to the arrival and assimilation of information that is nonuniform across trading and nontrading hours. Grossman [26] has shown that information is collected by traders as long as the expected gain from trading on the information exceeds the costs of producing that information. French and Roll [21] conduct an empirical analysis of the impact of information on the difference between trading and nontrading time stock return variance. French and Roll consider three possible explanations for the observed variance pattern. First, high trading-time variance is caused by public information, which is more likely to be released during normal business hours. Public information is information that becomes known to all market participants at the same time that it begins to affect prices (e.g., Supreme Court decisions, financial reports, governmental reports). Second, high trading-time variance is caused by private information, which is more likely to affect prices when the exchanges are open. This should occur because private information affects prices only through trading; thus, the production of private information may be more common when the exchanges are open. The benefits of producing private information are larger during the trading hours of the exchanges, when investors are able to trade on their private information. French and Roll also point out that even if the production rate of private information is constant, trades based on this type of information could lead to high trading-time variance. Private information that has been produced during the exchange nontrading hours cannot be acted upon until the exchanges are open. As a result, price reaction will not be apparent until the exchanges are open. The third explanation for the observed variance differential is that pricing errors induced by noise trading leads to high trading-time variance. To the extent that daily pricing errors occur during trading hours, these errors may increase the trading-time variance of stock returns.

To test the three hypotheses, French and Roll use daily close-to-close returns for all stocks listed on the New York Stock Exchange (NYSE) and American Stock Exchange (AMEX) between 1963 and 1982 to calculate stock return variances for weekdays, weekends, holidays, and holiday weekends. The average hourly variance when the NYSE is open is found to be approximately 72 percent higher than the hourly variance when the exchange is closed during the weekends. Exchanges' holidays (the NYSE and AMEX were closed on Wednesdays during the second half of 1968 due to a paperwork backlog) allow French and Roll to compare the exchange holiday variance (based on Tuesday-close to Thursday-close returns) with a normal weekday variance (e.g., Monday-close to Tuesday-close variance). The public information hypothesis predicts that the variance will not be reduced by the exchange holidays since the generation of public information should be a function of normal business hours and not of the exchange trading hours. According to the private information hypothesis, the variance will be reduced by the exchanges' holidays. Exchange holidays tend to reduce the value of private information, which needs to be acted upon before it becomes public. However, if the private information hypothesis is correct, then the reduction in variance should be temporary since some variance should be recovered on days immediately following exchange holidays.[4] Equivalently, the variance on days following exchange holidays should be higher than normal. The trading noise hypothesis, on the other hand, predicts that the reduction of variance on exchange holidays will be permanent.[5]

4. French and Roll also point out that in reality, most information falls between private and public categories. The private/public information artificial dichotomy is used only to facilitate their analysis. In addition, privately generated information eventually becomes public knowledge as it is disseminated through the trading process (see Goldman and Sosin [24]).

5. Whether trading on noise as if it were information is an important factor in security markets is an unsettled issue. The traditional view maintains that investors who trade on noise cannot survive in the long run (see, for example, Figlewski [20]). This view has been challenged in some recent theoretical studies. Black [4] argues that noise trading must account for a significant proportion of total trading in securities markets. Trueman [50] provides a theoretical model that describes investment managers who engaged in noise trading because the level of the managers' trading activity provides positive signals about their ability to collect information on current and potential investments. DeLong, Shleifer, Summers, and Waldman [15] argue that under certain assumptions, noise traders will survive and come to dominate the market in terms of wealth in the long run. The economic

French and Roll find the ratio of exchange holiday variance to a normal weekday variance to be consistent with both private information and noise trading hypotheses. On average, the two-day exchange holiday variance (Tuesday-close to Thursday-close) is only 14.5 percent higher than the variance for normal one-day returns. The overall results led French and Roll to conclude that the trading/nontrading time variance differential is caused by differences in the flow of information during the opening and closing hours of the major exchanges.[6] For the sample of stock returns examined, relatively low return variance over exchange holidays suggests that most of the information is private.

Other empirical studies have also shed some light on the pattern of asset return volatility and information arrival process. There is substantial empirical evidence that suggests that volatility of asset returns is significantly affected by the arrival of public information. French, Schwert, and Stambaugh [22] demonstrate that the *ex ante* risk premium on common stocks is positively related to the anticipated volatility of returns. Christie [10] and Kalay and Loewenstein [34] report that stock returns are more volatile around regularly scheduled news announcements. Moreover, if the news announcements are unanticipated, the uncertainty around the events can be even greater. Recently, Brown, Harlow, and Tinic [6] developed the uncertain information hypothesis as a means to explain the response of rational, risk-averse investors to the arrival of unanticipated information. The hypothesis predicts that following news of a dramatic financial event, both the risk and the expected return of the affected stocks can increase systematically. Although capital market rationality assumes that investors learn to make correct inferences about the impact of new information on the future distribution of returns (i.e., noisy rational expectation), it does not imply that prices react instantaneously to information. This should be the case since investors often set stock prices before they are completely certain about the full ramifications of a dra-

role of noise trading and its effect on volatility is not examined in this study. Empirical investigation of this issue is likely to require transactional data.

6. In a recent paper, Ross [46] also shows that in an arbitrage-free economy, the volatility of prices is directly related to the rate of flow of information to the market. In a simple model, the two were found to be identical (i.e., if the volatility of prices is not equal to the rate at which information arrives, then arbitrage is possible). An interesting point is that this result is independent of the asset pricing model that is used. This is consistent with the results reported in French and Roll [21]. According to Ross' arbitrage analysis, if prices are more volatile when markets are open for trading, then more information must be released when markets are open than when they are closed.

matic financial event. As a result, short-run price movements can exhibit increased volatility while the uncertainty about the full impact of the news is being resolved.

The present trend toward globally integrated financial markets has led to greater interest in research into the characteristics of distributional parameters for assets that are traded internationally. The effect of information arrival on trading and nontrading time variances for securities with international listings is examined in recent studies by Barclay, Litzenberger, and Warner [3], Hill, Schneeweis, and Yau [28], Makhija and Nachtman [39], and Savanayana, Schneeweis, and Yau [47]. Barclay et al. examine the effects of information and expanded trading hours on the return variance of U.S. stocks listed on the NYSE and the Tokyo Stock Exchange (TSE). For stocks that are traded on multiple markets, liquidity traders will concentrate their trading in the market with the lowest transaction costs (see also Admati and Pfleiderer [1]). For U.S. stocks traded in the United States and Japan, the transaction costs of liquidity traders should be lowest on the domestic NYSE. To the extent that informed investors tend to trade when trading by liquidity traders is concentrated, return variance measured during the NYSE trading hours should be positively associated with the higher trading volume on the NYSE. Comparing the daily trading time (open-to-close) and 24-hour (close-to-close) variances of U.S. dual-listed stocks with those of matched NYSE-listed U.S. stocks, the authors find no significant differences in the ratios of within-day to 24-hour variances between the two groups of stocks. Secondary listing of U.S. stocks in Japan does not appear to increase stock return variance. It should be pointed out, however, that although the results of Barclay et al. suggest that the magnitude of the total variance may not change, the distribution of return variance can be affected by the trading on the TSE. Since news with significant impact on stocks often is released after the close of the NYSE, it is possible that a nontrivial fraction of the overnight return variance of the dual-listed stocks is actually caused by investors' trading on the TSE in reaction to the after-hours new releases in the United States. For some information whose value declines rapidly with time, some investors (e.g., nonliquidity traders) may find it beneficial to trade on the TSE despite higher liquidity and lower average transaction costs on the NYSE.[7]

7. Theoretical frameworks modeling stock trading behavior as developed by Kyle [37] and Admati and Pfleiderer [1] focus on information that is privately acquired. Variance is associated with the trading reaction of informed investors and liquidity traders to each other (i.e., trade generates trade).

Barclay et al. also report that on average the variance of the cross-listed stocks during the NYSE trading hours is greater than the variance during the TSE trading hours. Although the reported differential in trading time variances may reflect the larger trading volume of these stocks on the NYSE, the higher variance during NYSE trading hours is also consistent with the hypothesis that the volatility of asset returns is related to the majority of relevant public information being released during the hours of the primary exchange.

In a similar study, Makhija and Nachtman [39] assess the effect of expanded trading time on the daily close-to-close return variances of 81 stocks cross-listed on the NYSE and the London Stock Exchange (LSE) from 1969 to 1982. Contrary to Barclay et al.'s findings on the impact of TSE listing on the 24-hour variance of NYSE–TSE cross-listed stocks, Makhija and Nachtman report a significant increase in the 24-hour (U.S. close-to-close) return variance of NYSE–LSE cross-listed stocks following the listing on the LSE. Those authors conclude that the opportunity to trade on the LSE induces investors to acquire additional information. Viewing information as a store of volatility, greater production of information leads to an increase in return variance after cross-listings. In sum, although the studies by Makhija and Nachtman and Barclay, Litzenberger, and Warner [3] have not fully considered the time pattern of variance across various trading and nontrading periods in international markets (i.e., trading and nontrading time variances that are based on opening and closing prices from different markets), they provide evidence that suggests that the effects of information and trading in international stock markets on stock return variance may differ for various foreign markets in which the stocks are listed.

The impact of information arrival on price movements has also been investigated for the foreign exchange markets. Worldwide foreign exchange trading takes place on a 24-hour basis. In two related studies, Ito and Roley [30, 31] examine the impacts of news announcements on the yen/dollar spot rate movements. In the first study [30], the authors document the characteristics of yen/dollar movements in four intraday disaggregated segments from 1980 through 1985. These segments are (1) New York-open to New York-close, (2) New York-close to Tokyo-open, (3) Tokyo-open to Tokyo-close, and (4) Tokyo-close to New York-open. The results indicate that the New York market was generally more volatile, perhaps reflecting more relevant news. Among the economic announcements considered, Ito and Roley find that U.S. money supply announcement surprises had the most consistent effects, especially prior to 1984. Positive surprises were found to result in dollar appreciation. Other U.S. announcements had effect only in the post-February 1984 period, which could reflect the change in emphasis by the Federal Reserve Bank and traders from money supply to economic activity. For Japanese economic announcements, only industrial production new exhibits impact on the rate movements.

In a recent paper, Hill, Schneeweis, and Yau [28] provide some empirical evidence that suggests that the variance of the internationally traded U.S. Treasury bond futures and Eurodollar futures price changes are nonconstant across various trading and nontrading periods. In addition, Hill et al. show that the variance of price changes is lowest during the period in which the U.S. Treasury bond futures contracts are not traded on any international market. As an extension of Hill et al.'s study, Savanayana, Schneeweis, and Yau [47] test for the relative impacts of macroeconomic information generated in international markets (e.g., U.S. and Japanese information) on the trading/nontrading time variance pattern for the U.S. Treasury bond futures. Their results suggest that in addition to U.S. information, Japanese information affecting interest rates may have significant impact on the volatility of U.S. Treasury bond futures price movements during the period that Japanese information is released (Japanese business hours). Nonstationarity in the distribution of variances of U.S. Treasury bond futures appears to be a function of not only domestic information flows, but also relevant information generated in foreign countries.

Thus, evidence generally indicates the existence of lower variances during nontrading periods of U.S. markets. Because of the relative lack of information or the increased cost of transactions during nontrading hours, volatility during nontrading hours should be of a smaller magnitude than that during trading hours. The exact nature of return/risk relationships that exist during trading and nontrading periods cannot easily be modeled *ex ante* or be extended to non-U.S. markets since each trading and nontrading session is affected by the unique information set available in that time period.[8] For instance, due to the relative importance of U.S. dollars,

---

8. Associations between information, volume of trade, price level, return, and volatility have also been examined in several studies (for example, Cornell [11]; Jain and Joh [32]; Karpoff [35]). The link between volume and information, however, remains unclear. Using simulation methods, Karpoff shows that the relation between volume and information is affected by the institutional design of the market.

information about U.S. dollars released during U.S. trading periods may have a greater impact on prices of assets in foreign countries than information released during a foreign country's trading hours. Likewise, information released internally within a country may also be reflected during a particular nontrading time period if the market participants do not have time to react to the information during the trading hours of the local exchange. In the following sections we extend the analysis of trading/nontrading time and information effects to that of the French Notionelle futures contract. Analysis of futures markets may more easily capture the impact of information releases since futures markets have been shown to have lower transaction and investment costs, which enables it to reflect information in a more timely fashion [38].

III. MARKET STRUCTURE, DATA AND METHODOLOGY

(A) MATIF

The MATIF, France's futures market, has recently celebrated its third birthday. From 1987 through 1989, 33.3 million contracts have been traded, putting the MATIF in third place among the world's futures markets behind Chicago and Tokyo. The most successful of the contracts is the futures contract based on the Notionelle 10-year government bond. This contract has developed into an essential tool for French institutions. The range of potential strategies for the Notionelle futures contract is as broad as those for contracts in U.S. and other foreign futures contracts. (See Aftalion and Poncet [2] for a full discussion of the MATIF and the use of futures contracts.) The principal uses of futures, however, have been for risk minimization and asset risk/return management. During the period of analysis considered in this study, the hours of the MATIF are 10:00 A.M. to 3:00 P.M. French time (approximately 4:00 A.M. to 9:00 A.M. New York time).[9] This study primarily considers the risk pattern of the French Notionelle futures contract over trading time and nontrading times; however, the study also examines the impact of relevant infor-

---

9. An identical contract to the MATIF Notionelle is also traded on an over-the-counter basis outside exchange hours and is cleared and guaranteed by the clearinghouse. Due to lack of consistent trading liquidity and volume, this market is regarded as part of the nontrading period. If available, data from this market could, however, be used to more clearly test the impact of intraday pricing patterns.

mation release days on trading time and nontrading time risk measures. In France, money supply announcements are generally made between the fifth and tenth days of the month at 8:30 A.M. Likewise, French trade balance figures are usually reported in morning hours before the opening of the MATIF. Release times are obtained from S. G. Warburg International Economic Calendar.

(B) Data and Methodology

In this paper we focus on empirical evidence of the differences in variance of price changes during the trading and nontrading hours of the French Notionelle futures contract.[10] Daily opening and closing prices are used to calculate the variances for the trading and nontrading periods of the contract. The time period chosen in this analysis is November 17, 1986, to April 27, 1989. The near-term contract is used and is rolled over to the next near-term contract at the end of the month prior to the delivery month. The price data is obtained from Goldman Sachs, Inc., and the MATIF. The entire period is broken into three subperiods, each of which is analyzed separately. The methodology used in this analysis to compare estimated variances is similar to that described in Dyl and Maberly [17], Hill, Schneeweis, and Yau [28], and Savanayana, Schneeweis, and Yau [47].

IV. RESULTS

The variances of price changes for the French Notionelle futures contract over trading (daytime open-to-close) and nontrading (overnight close-to-open) intervals are reported for four time periods: (1) November 17, 1986, to April 27, 1989, (2) November 17, 1986, to September 4, 1987, (3) September 7, 1987, to June 22, 1988, and (4) June 23, 1988, to April 27, 1989. Results are presented in Table 1 for the overall November 17, 1986, to April 27, 1989, period and in Tables 2, 3, and 4 for subperiods 2, 3, and 4, respectively. Results are also reported graphically in Figures 1–2. The trading time hypothesis predicts that the variances of the trading periods would be equal. Moreover, since the hypothesis maintains that the return-generating process operates during

---

10. Other surrogates for asset risk and price movement also exist, for example, semivariance and semideviation; however, it has been shown that there exists a high correlation between variance and other commonly used surrogates for security risk.

Table 1
French Notionelle futures contract means and variances of price changes over trading and nontrading periods, 11/17/86–4/27/89

Time Period:	Whole Period	Mon.	Tues.	Wed.	Thurs.	Fri.
Trading Time u :	−.003	−.092	.046	−.016	−.012	.064
σ^2:	.129	.100	.141	.124	.156	.141
Nontrading Time u :	−.008	−.042	.025	.020	.012	.020
σ^2:	.223[a]	.218[a]	.187	.140	.236	.348[a]

[a]Using standard F-test comparisons, the variance of the nontrading period is significantly greater than the variance of the trading period at the .10 level.

trading hours only, the variances of price changes would tend to be larger over trading periods than over nontrading periods. The calendar time hypothesis suggests that the variances of the trading (nontrading) periods would be a strict multiple of the hours in each trading (nontrading) period. An informational hypothesis would suggest that the magnitude of variance would be a function of the information activity in each time period.

Table 2
French Notionelle futures contract means and variances of price changes over trading and nontrading periods, 11/17/86–9/4/87

Time Period:	Whole Period	Mon.	Tues.	Wed.	Thurs.	Fri.
Trading Time u :	−.026	−.069	−.050	−.003	−.015	.011
σ^2:	.112	.097	.126	.135	.108	.100
Nontrading Time u :	−.011	−.064	−.040	.050	.010	−.007
σ^2:	.114	.093	.132	.114	.080	.348[a]

[a]Using standard F-test comparisons, the variance of the nontrading period is significantly greater than the variance of the trading period at the .10 level.

Trading Time: Open MATIF$_t$ to close MATIF$_t$.

Nontrading Time: Close MATIF$_t$ to open MATIF$_{t+1}$.

Table 3

French Notionelle futures contract means and variances of price changes over trading and nontrading periods, 9/7/87–6/22/87

Time Period:	Whole Period	Mon.	Tues.	Wed.	Thurs.	Fri.
Trading Time u :	.008	−.154	.120	−.026	−.050	.185
σ^2:	.239	.157	.243	.222	.326	.215
Nontrading Time u :	.021	−.099	.106	.077	.005	.065
σ^2:	.439[a]	.516[a]	.358	.156	.354	.641[a]
(Excluding 10 / 7 / 87–10 / 26 / 87)						
Trading Time σ^2:	.139	.106	.132	.084	.169	.189
Nontrading Time σ^2:	.249[a]	.190	.280[a]	.129	.382[a]	.231

[a]Using standard F-test comparisons, the variance of the nontrading period is significantly greater than the variance of the trading period at the .10 level of significance.

For security markets, the information hypothesis implies that the greatest variances will exist during a market's trading time (the period from the opening to the closing of a market). However, for a foreign capital market, information released in U.S. markets during the nontrading time of the foreign capital market may have a greater impact on that country's domestic security prices than information released during trading time in the home country. For instance, information releases on U.S. GNP, trade balance, and interest rates may have a greater impact on the demand for French securities than would certain French domestic economic information releases. If this differential impact exists, higher variance would be expected during the period for which the U.S. markets are open. Results as shown in Tables 1–4 are consistent with this relative information effect.[11] As shown in the analysis of the French Notionelle futures contract data in Table 1, the periods with the highest variances are non-

11. Our results are generally not consistent with the primary predictions of either the calendar time or trading time hypothesis. The weekend variance (Friday-close to Monday-close) is only 1.3 times the average weekday variance (e.g., Tuesday-close to Wednesday-close). The calendar time and trading time hypotheses would predict the ratio of weekend variance to average weekday variance to be 3 and 1, respectively.

Table 4
French Notionelle futures contract means and variances of price changes over trading and nontrading periods, 6/23/88–4/27/89

Time Period:	Whole Period	Mon.	Tues.	Wed.	Thurs.	Fri.
Trading Time u :	.005	.053	.067	–.019	.025	–.007
σ^2:	.056	.045	.050	.028	.050	.108
Nontrading Time u :	.002	.039	.011	–.059	.021	.008
σ^2:	.101[a]	.046	.076	.145[a]	.096	.122

[a]Using standard F-test comparisons, the variance of the nontrading period is significantly greater than the variance of the trading period at the .10 level of significance.

Trading Time: Open $MATIF_t$ to close $MATIF_t$.

Nontrading Time: Close $MATIF_t$ to open $MATIF_{t+1}$.

trading periods, which encompass the principal part of the U.S. and Japanese trading hours. These results are consistent across all weekdays (Monday through Friday). For the entire period of November 17, 1986, to April 27, 1989, the variance of price changes during the trading period was 0.129. In contrast, the variance of price changes during the nontrading period was 0.223 for the same period. In Tables 2–4 we present the trading and nontrading time variances of price changes for the subperiods November 17, 1986, to September 4, 1987; September 7, 1987, to June 22, 1988; and June 23, 1988, to April 27, 1989, respectively. Results similar to those in Table 1 are obtained; that is, for the French Notionelle futures contract, the variances of price changes over nontrading periods tend to exceed those of trading periods.

It is important to point out that in all three subperiods, results do not consistently indicate a greater variance in the nontrading period on all days of the week. For unique time periods on certain days, information released in France may have a greater impact on price variability than information released in the United States or Japan. The effect of information on trading and nontrading time variances should therefore be determined by the nature and timing of individual information releases.[12]

Figure 1
Standard deviations of price changes for French Notionelle futures contract for the period 11/17/86–4/27/89 (Figure 1a) and 11/17/86–9/4/87 (Figure 1b)

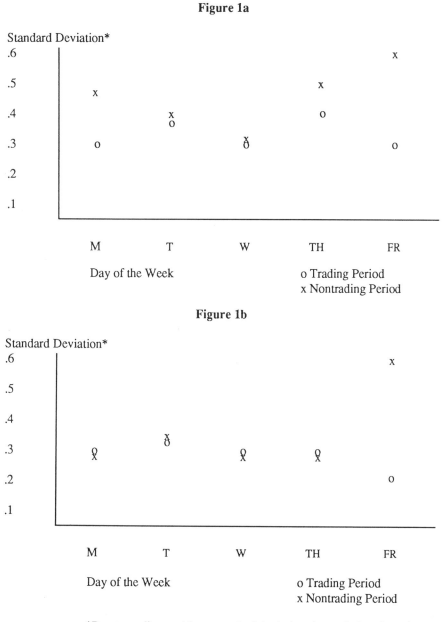

Figure 1a

Standard Deviation*

Figure 1b

Standard Deviation*

*Due to scaling problem, standard deviations instead of variances are used in graphical presentation.

Figure 2
Standard deviations of price changes for French Notionelle futures contract for the period 9/7/87–6/22/88 (Figure 2a) and 6/23/88–4/27/86 (Figure 2b)

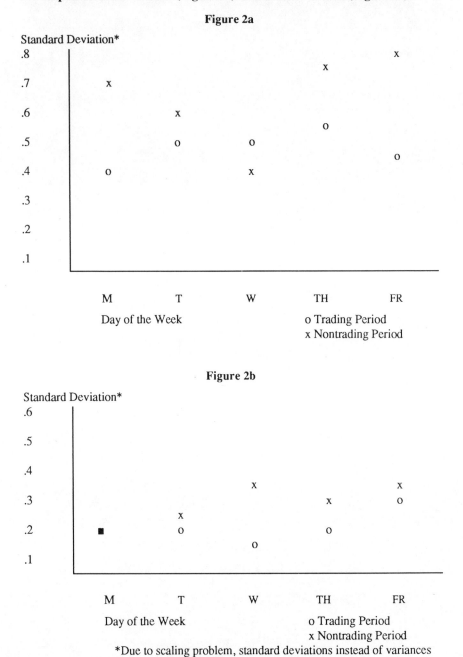

Figure 2a

Standard Deviation*

.8					x
				x	
.7	x				
.6		x			
				o	
.5		o	o		
					o
.4	o		x		
.3					
.2					
.1					

M   T   W   TH   FR

Day of the Week   o Trading Period
                         x Nontrading Period

Figure 2b

Standard Deviation*

.6					
.5					
.4					
			x		x
.3				x	o
		x			
.2	■	o		o	
			o		
.1					

M   T   W   TH   FR

Day of the Week   o Trading Period
                         x Nontrading Period

*Due to scaling problem, standard deviations instead of variances are used in graphical presentation.

Table 5

French Notionelle futures contract means and variances of price changes over trading and nontrading time periods for french money supply (MS) and trade balance (TB) announcements days during the period of 5/4/87–4/27/89 (excluding 10/7/87–10/26/87)

Time Period:	Whole Period Excluding MS and TB Days	MS Days Only	TB Days Only
Trading Time σ^2:	.103	.058	.084
Nontrading Time σ^2:	.167	.050	.088

To test the proposition that some French information releases can lead to the variance's being greater during the trading hours of the MATIF on certain days, we examine the impact of French money supply and trade balance announcements on the pattern of variances for the Notionelle futures contract. In Table 5 the trading and nontrading time variances are given separately for the entire period of November 17, 1986, to April 27, 1989, excluding French money supply and trade balance announcement days as well as for days during this period on which money supply and trade balance announcements are made. Results from Table 5 indicate that in contrast to the overall trading and nontrading time variances (0.103/0.167), on days that the French money supply and trade balance information is released, the variances of the trading and nontrading times are similar (0.058/0.050 for money supply days and 0.084/0.088 for trade balance days).[13]

12. Private information may also affect variance. However, the amount of private information on government securities is probably very limited. In addition, as pointed out by Kyle [37], public information also acts as a substitute for private information that is not traded on.

13. Investors' timing of trades may also be affected by an individual firm's or country's timing of information releases. The timing of information releases must be considered in trading cycles. For instance, to the degree that the French economic information releases precede the opening of the French MATIF, the impact of the releases will be captured in the preceding nontrading time. Although information impacts include both anticipated and unanticipated portions, we would expect to detect an increase in volatility in a surrounding period as long as investors differ in their individual analysis of the eventual impact of a particular information release. The impact of unanticipated information could be assessed in future studies by employing consensus forecasts provided by firms such as MMS International. It should be noted that for the European markets, MMS International has increased significantly the number of economic information variables offered for the European markets.

Table 6
French Notionelle futures contract means and variances of price changes over trading and nontrading periods for 11/17/86–4/27/89 (excluding 10/7/87–10/26/87)

Time Period:	Whole Period	Mon.	Tues.	Wed.	Thurs.	Fri.
Trading Time σ^2:	.104	.087	.106	.081	.109	.137
Nontrading Time σ^2:	.171	.116	.166	.135	.188	.244

Trading Time: Open MATIF_t to close MATIF_t.

Nontrading Time: Close MATIF_t to open MATIF_{t+1}.

It is important to note that the analysis of trading/nontrading time effect on variances may also be affected by unique time periods. The time period used in this analysis includes the great October 1987 crash. When the two-week period surrounding the crash is removed, results for the subperiod of September 7, 1987, to June 22, 1988 (Table 3) show that the variances changed from 0.239 to 0.139 for the trading time and from 0.439 to 0.249 for the nontrading time. Trading and nontrading time variances for the entire period (November 17, 1986, to April 27, 1989) excluding the two-week period surrounding the crash are given in Table 6. Even with the crash period removed, results still indicate that the variance over the trading time is less than that estimated for the nontrading time period. [14]

14. A final comment should be made on the stationarity of the variance over the three years examined. For the French Notionelle futures contract, the reported variances for the three subperiods were not significantly different. The trading-time variances for the subperiods were, respectively, 0.112, 0.139 (crash excluded), and 0.056. The variances for nontrading periods were, respectively, 0.114, 0.249 (crash excluded), and 0.101. However, it is important to note that the trading time and nontrading time variances of the final subperiod are less than those of either the first or second subperiod. These results may indicate that the variability of price changes may be decreasing in both the French and the overseas markets. In addition, it could be expected that for a period near the beginning of the Notionelle contract trading and during the period surrounding the crash, a lack of liquidity and high trading costs may have resulted in wider price swings.

V. SUMMARY AND IMPLICATIONS

Several hypotheses have been advanced for the higher volatility of asset returns during trading time period compared to nontrading time period. These hypotheses include information flows [21], market structure [24], and security settlement procedures [33]. Today, certain securities can be traded around the clock during weekdays as well as into the weekend hours. Some securities are traded 24 hours a day (e.g., Foreign Exchange). Moreover, new financial markets are coming into existence. Financial futures markets recently have begun in England, France and Germany, and are soon to start in Spain and Italy. One of the principal economic base for futures markets is their importance in price discovery (reflecting new information). Tests on the trading/nontrading time effect in futures markets as well as the impact of information flows on the volatility of futures prices in these markets are required.

In this paper, we examine the pattern of the volatility of the French Notionelle futures contract price changes across trading and nontrading periods of the MATIF. In addition, we test for the impact of information releases believed to be particularly important to interest rate markets in France on relative trading and nontrading time variances. In contrast to results for U.S. markets, for the period analyzed reported variances of the French Notionelle futures contract price changes were often greater over nontrading time periods.[15] Several reasons may explain the differential results relative to U.S. markets. Information flow during the MATIF trading hours may, on average, have smaller impact on the French bond markets than information generated during a U.S. or Japanese trading session. A security's risk as measured by variance is not a strict function of calendar time or trading time, but of information arrival and the expected impact of that information. If U.S. banks engage in interest rate arbitrage between U.S. and French rates, any changes in U.S. rates during

---

15. Although results of the public, private, and noise information tests are not reported in this paper, empirical analysis similar to that conducted by French and Roll [21] was completed. Variances of price changes over exchange holidays and the trading period following exchange holidays were compared in order to test for the relative impacts of private and public information. In contrast to French and Roll, our exchange holidays may coincide with national holidays. The variance of the exchange holiday nontrading period was greater than that of the following trading period (9.6 percent versus 6.8 percent). These results do not support either a pure public information or a private information hypothesis. In fact, due to the increasing ease of trading off market, tests of private versus public information may be inconclusive. Moreover, French and Roll themselves stated that in their study the private versus public information dichotomy was an artificial one.

U.S. trading hours may have immediate impact on French bonds during the nontrading period of the French markets. Results, as shown in the Appendix, however, also indicate that the differential between trading and nontrading time variances in the French Notionelle futures contract may be decreasing. This convergence of trading and nontrading time variances may reflect increasing liquidity and falling transaction costs in the French MATIF. Equally important, on days when certain French public macroinformation (money supply and trade balance figures) is released, the variances of price changes for the Notionelle futures contract are similar over the trading hours and nontrading hours of the MATIF. These French macroinformation releases seemingly affect the French domestic market in a similar fashion to how U.S. macroinformation releases affect U.S. security markets.[16]

Results from this study have implications for various trading strategies as well as for the design of market structures. If variance is nonstationary during the day, models based on this risk measure must likewise adjust for the changing variance. In addition, the French MATIF may wish to increase its trading hours to directly incorporate the times of the domestic information releases instead of relying on over-the-counter trades. Likewise, the French markets may wish to offer extended trading hours to include periods in which foreign information, particularly important to the French market, is made public.

Further tests should be conducted on the relative importance of different types of information generated in various countries. The significance of particular macroinformation may well be country-dependent. As important, studies that concentrate on the impact of firm-specific information may need to consider macroinformation being released during trading and nontrading periods in other markets.[17] Future research is required to determine the relative impact of the macroeconomic and firm-specific

16. In the Appendix we report for the last four three-month periods the variances during trading and nontrading times. Results indicate that for the last two periods (November 18, 1988, to January 30, 1989, and January 31, 1989, to April 27, 1989), the trading- and nontrading-time variances are not significantly different. Readers may note, however, that the trading-time variances during the last three months are greater than those during previous three-month trading-time periods. For similar information, a higher variance may be observed in a more liquid market due to lower transaction costs. Research is required to determine if changes in volatility as measured by variances are due to unique information or changing transaction costs.

17. The focus of this study is on the pure information effect on volatility pattern of the French Notionelle futures contract. Future research should also examine the characteristics of internal market dynamics such as the variance spillover effect between markets.

information in various markets and the degree to which the globalization of markets results in similar information reaction across countries.

REFERENCES

1. Admati, A., and P. Pfleiderer. 1987. "A Theory of Intraday Trading Patterns." Research Paper #927, Stanford University, Graduate School of Business.
2. Aftalion, F., and P. Poncet. 1986. *Le Matif*. Presses Universitaires de France.
3. Barclay, M., R. Litzenberger, and J. Warner. 1988. "Private Information, Trading Volumes and Stock Return Variances." Working Paper, University of Rochester.
4. Black, F. 1986. "Noise." *Journal of Finance* (July), 529–543.
5. Bollerslev, T. 1986. "Generalized Autoregressive Conditional Heteroskedasticity." *Journal of Econometrics* 31, 307–327.
6. Brown, K., W. Harlow, and S. Tinic. 1988. "Risk Aversion, Uncertain Information, and Market Efficiency." *Journal of Financial Economics* 22, 355–385.
7. Castanias, R. 1979. "Macroeconomic Information and the Variability of Stock Market Prices." *Journal of Finance* (May), 439–450.
8. Chen, N., R. Roll, and S. Ross. 1986. "Economic Forces and the Stock Market." *Journal of Business* (July), 383–403.
9. Chiang, R. C., and T. C. Tapley. 1982. "Day of the Week Effects and the Futures Markets." *Review of Research in Futures Markets* 2, no. 3, 356–410.
10. Christie, A. 1983. "On the Informational Arrival and Hypothesis Testing in Event Studies." Working Paper, University of Rochester, Graduate School of Management.
11. Cornell, B. 1981. "The Relationships between Volume and Price Variability in Futures Markets." *The Journal of Futures Markets*, no. 1 (Fall), 303–316.
12. Cornell, B. 1983. "Money Supply Announcements and Interest Rates: Another View." *Journal of Business* 56, no. 1, 1–23.
13. Cornell, B. 1985. "The Weekly Pattern in Stock Returns: Cash versus Futures: A Note." *Journal of Finance* (June), 583–588.
14. DeBondt, W., and R. Thaler. 1985. "Does the Stock Market Overreact?" *Journal of Finance* (July), 793–805.
15. DeLong, J. B., A. Shleifer, L. Summers, and R. Waldman. 1988. "The Survival of Noise Trader in Financial Market." National Bureau of Economic Research, Working Paper No. 2715.
16. Deravi, K., P. Gregorowicz, and C. Hegji. 1988. "Balance of Trade Announcements and Movements in Exchange Rates." *Southern Economic Journal* 55, no. 2 (October), 279–287.
17. Dyl, E., and E. Maberly. 1986. "The Weekly Pattern in Stock Index Futures: A Further Note." *Journal of Finance* (December), 1149–1152.
18. Engle, R., T. Ito, and W. Lin. "Meteor Showers or Heat Wave? Heteroskedastic Intra-Daily Volatility in the Foreign Exchange Market." National Bureau of Economic Research, Working Paper No. 2609.
19. Fama, E. 1965. "The Behavior of Stock Market Price." *Journal of Business* 38, no. 1, 34–105.
20. Figlewski, S. 1979. "Market Efficiency in a Market with Heterogeneous Information." *Journal of Political Economy* 86, 581–597.
21. French, K., and R. Roll. 1986. "Stock Return Variance: The Arrival of Information and the Reaction of Traders." *Journal of Financial Economics* 17, 5–26.
22. French, K., G. Schwert, and R. Stambaugh. 1987. "Expected Stock Returns and Volatility," *Journal of Financial Economics* 19, 3–29.

23. Garman, M. B., and M. S. Klass. 1980. "On the Estimation of Security Price Volatilities from Historical Data." *Journal of Business* 53, no. 1, 67–78.
24. Goldman, M., and H. Sosin. 1979. "Information Dissemination, Market Efficiency and the Frequency of Transactions." *Journal of Financial Economics* 7, 29–61.
25. Grossman, S., and J. Stiglitz. 1980. "On the Impossibility of Informationally Efficient Markets." *The American Economic Review* (June), 393–408.
26. Grossman, S. F. 1979. "Rational Expectations and the Allocation of Resources under Asymmetric Information: A Survey." Working Paper, University of Pennsylvania.
27. Harris, L. 1986. "A Transaction Data Study of Weekly and Intradaily Patterns in Stock Returns." *Journal of Financial Economics* 16, 99–117.
28. Hill, J., T. Schneeweis, and J. Yau. 1988. "International Trading/Non-Trading Time Effect on Risk Estimation in Futures Markets." Paper presented at a meeting of the Financial Management Association.
29. Ito, T. "The Intradaily Exchange Rate Dynamics and Monetary Policies after the G–5 Agreement." National Bureau of Economic Research, Working Paper No. 2048.
30. Ito, T., and V. Roley. 1986. "News from the U.S. and Japan: Which Moves the Yen/Dollar Exchange Rate?" Research Paper, Federal Reserve Bank of Kansas City (July).
31. Ito, T., and V. Roley. 1988. "Intraday Yen/Dollar Exchange Rate Movements: News or Noise." Research Paper, Federal Reserve Bank of Kansas City (October).
32. Jain, P., and G. Joh. 1988. "The Dependence between Hourly Prices and Trading Volume." *Journal of Financial and Quantitative Analysis* 23, no. 3 (September), 269–283.
33. Jordan, J., W. Seale, S. Dinehart, and D. Kenyon. 1988. "The Intraday Variability of Soybean Futures Prices: Information and Trading Effects." *The Review of Futures Markets* 7, no. 1, 96–107.
34. Kalay, A., and U. Loewenstein. 1985. "Predictable Events and Excess Returns: The Case of Dividend Announcements." *Journal of Financial Economics* 14, 423–449.
35. Karpoff, J. 1986. "A Theory of Trading Volume." *Journal of Finance* (December), 1069–1087.
36. Keim, D. B., and R. F. Stambaugh. 1984. "A Further Investigation of the Weekend Effects in Stock Returns." *Journal of Finance* (July), 433–454.
37. Kyle, A. 1984. "Informational Efficiency and Liquidity in a Continuous Auction Futures Market." Working Paper, Columbia Business School, Center for the Study of Futures Markets.
38. Mackinlay, A. Craig, and Ramaswamy, K. 1988. "Index-Futures Arbitrage and the Behavior of Stock Index Futures Prices." *The Review of Financial Studies* (September), 137–158.
39. Makhija, A., and R. Nachtman. 1989. "Empirical Evidence on Alternative Theories of Stock Return Variances: The Effects of Expanded Trading Time on NYSE–LSE Cross Listed Stocks." Working Paper, University of Pittsburgh (January).
40. Marsh, T., and R. Webb. 1983. "Informational Dissemination Uncertainty, the Continuity of Trading and the Structure of International Futures Markets." *Review of Research in Futures Markets* 2, no. 1, 36–71.
41. Martell, T., and A. Wolf. 1985. "Determinants of Trading Volume in Futures Markets." Working Paper, Columbia Business School, Center for the Study of Futures Markets (July).
42. Merrick, J. 1986. "Volume Determination in Stock Index Futures of Markets: An Analysis of Arbitrage and Volatility Effects." Working Paper, New York University (April).
43. Oldfield, G. S., Jr., and R. J. Rogalski. 1980. "A Theory of Common Stock Returns over Trading and Non-Trading Periods." *Journal of Finance* (June), 729–752.
44. Parkinson, M. 1980. "The Extreme Value Method for Estimating the Variance of the Rate of Return." *Journal of Business* 53, no. 1, 61–65.
45. Phillips-Patrick, F., and T. Schneeweis. 1988. "The 'Weekend Effect' for Stock Indexes and

Stock Index Futures: Dividend and Interest Rate Effects." *The Journal of Futures Markets* (February), 115–121.

46. Ross, S. A. 1989. "Information and Volatility: The No-Arbitrage Martingale Approach to Timing and Resolution Irrelevancy." *Journal of Finance* (March), 1–17.

47. Savanayana, U., T. Schneeweis, and J. Yau. 1989. "Trading/Non-Trading Time and Information Effects in U.S. Treasury Bond Futures Market." Working Paper, University of Massachusetts, Amherst.

48. Shiller, R. 1984. "Stock Prices and Social Dynamics." *Brookings Papers on Economic Activity* 2, 457–498.

49. Summers, L. 1986. "Does the Stock Market Rationally Reflect Fundamental Values." *Journal of Finance* (July), 591–601.

50. Trueman, B. 1988. "A Theory of Noise Trading in Securities Markets." *Journal of Finance* (March), 83–95.

Appendix

French Notionelle futures contract variances of price changes, 6/23/88–9/22/88

Time Period:	Whole Period	Mon.	Tues.	Wed.	Thurs.	Fri.
Trading Time u :	.007	−.087	.080	−.015	−.036	.100
σ²:	.043	.086ᵃ	.058	.020	.031	.020
Nontrading Time u :	−.037	.050	.020	−.260	−.009	.044
σ²:	.094ᵃ	.032	.126ᵃ	.207ᵃ	.038	.011

ᵃUsing standard F-test comparisons, the variance of the nontrading period is significantly greater than that of the trading period at the .10 level.

French Notionelle futures contract variances of price changes, 9/6/88–11/17/88

Time Period:	Whole Period	Mon.	Tues.	Wed.	Thurs.	Fri.
Trading Time u :	.035	−.044	.035	−.027	.095	.138
σ²:	.051	.038	.020	.019	.091	.093
Nontrading Time u :	.036	.128	−.070	.091	.020	.062
σ²:	.132ᵃ	.032	.052ᵃ	.181ᵃ	.141	.299ᵃ

ᵃUsing standard F-test comparisons, the variance of the nontrading period is significantly greater than that of the trading period at the .10 level.

French Notionelle futures contract variances of price changes, 11/18/88–1/30/89

Time Period:	Whole Period	Mon.	Tues.	Wed.	Thurs.	Fri.
Trading Time u :	.007	−.067	.060	−.043	−.008	−.020
σ²:	.033	.029	.039	.023	.041	.035
Nontrading Time u :	−.011	−.071	.077	−.095	.033	−.002
σ²:	.054	.029	.069	.073ᵃ	.031	.070ᵃ

ᵃUsing standard F-test comparisons, the variance of the nontrading period is significantly greater than that of the trading period at the .10 level.

French Notionelle futures contract variances of price changes, 1/31/89–4/27/89

Time Period:	Whole Period	Mon.	Tues.	Wed.	Thurs.	Fri.
Trading Time u :	−.025	−.024	.086	−.062	.037	−.180
σ^2:	.085	.046	.083	.045	.047	.204
Nontrading Time u :	.016	.047	.018	−.005	.072	−.049
σ^2:	.108	.077	.071	.099[a]	.183[a]	.142

[a]Using standard F-test comparisons, the variance of the nontrading period is significantly greater than that of the trading period at the .10 level.

Comments

MICHAEL J. BARCLAY*

This paper adds to the growing literature on the relation between trading and nontrading time variances. Several recent studies, including French and Roll (1986) and Barclay, Litzenberger, and Warner (1990), find that the returns on common stock have higher variances during exchange trading hours than during nontrading hours. This result has been attributed in part to private information that is revealed through trading. Geman, Savanayana, and Schneeweis conduct a related test by examining the trading-day and overnight variance of the French Notionelle futures contract, an actively traded futures contract for 10-year French government bonds. In contrast to the results in previous studies, price changes for the French Notionelle futures contract have higher variance during the overnight period than during the French trading day.

The replication of results using new data from different markets, at different times, and from different countries is a vital part of the scientific process. Only through replication can we gain confidence in the robustness of our empirical findings. During this process, however, it is important not to forget the inherent differences between markets and between countries that will lead to differences in results. In these comments I focus on the differences between this paper and those that precede it, rather than on the similarities.

The most dramatic innovation in the Geman et al. paper is their focus on the government bond market instead of the equities market. This difference is likely to be important for several reasons. First, as mentioned above, much of the difference between the trading and nontrading time variances in equity markets has been attributed to the release of private information through trading. If this hypothesis is correct, then the implications about the government bond market depend critically on the nature of informed traders' private information. If private information consists primarily of marketwide factors such as inflation or real business cycle activity, then we might expect trading to affect the variance of bond prices in much the same way that it affects the variance of equity prices.

*Simon Graduate School of Business Administration, University of Rochester.

If, on the other hand, private information is largely firm- or industry-specific, then trading should not affect the volatility of bond prices. Barclay et al. examine the nature of private information revealed through trading in equity markets by examining the effect of trading on individual stocks, industry indexes, and a market index. They find that private information contains firm-specific, industrywide, and marketwide components. Since the marketwide component of private information is a relatively small fraction of the total, however, we should expect a correspondingly smaller effect of trading on the return variance in the government bond market than in the equity market.

The second major difference between the government bond market and the equity market is the ability of traders to trade when the primary market is closed. If I have private information that a particular U.S. stock is under- or overvalued, it may be virtually impossible for me to trade on that information when the U.S. market is closed. Certainly, some U.S. stocks are traded overseas, but this number is small. Thus, we would expect most of the private information about common stocks to be revealed through trading on the domestic market. In the bond market, however, it is possible to replicate the payoffs to a French government bond whenever any of the world's major financial markets are open. If the U.S. market is open, for example, one can purchase a U.S. government bond with the appropriate maturity and then swap the dollar cash flows for French franc cash flows through the spot and forward exchange rate markets. Arbitragers prevent any significant price differential between this synthetically created French bond and the actual French government bond. Since the actual or the synthetic French government bond can be traded at any time, day or night, one would expect the bond-return variance during the French trading day to reflect only its share of the 24-hour trading day.

The relation between international default-free interest rates generated through arbitrage restrictions in the government bond and the foreign exchange markets raises a third major difference between the government bond and the equities markets. Default-free interest rates are determined in the world market. Intercountry differences in rates are minimized by capital flows from lower-return to higher-return countries. Thus, information concerning interest rates in the other major financial centers, such as the United States or Japan, may have a greater effect on the French Notionelle futures contract than information disclosed in France. This is much less the case in the equity markets. Although multinational corporations are significantly affected by conditions abroad, for many firms the most relevant information concerns the demand and supply conditions in their domestic market. Both public and private information about these conditions is generated at a faster rate during the domestic trading day.

Finally, to examine the effect of trading on return variances, it is important to control for other factors that affect variance, most notably the release of public information. Both French and Roll and Barclay et al. attempt to identify trading and nontrading periods during which the flow of public information is expected to be roughly the same. Although there may be an analogous experiment in the government bond market, the nature of that experiment is not obvious. Thus, interpretation of the results in this paper is difficult because it seems impossible to separate the effects of trading per se from the release of public information and other factors that generate variance.

To summarize, Geman et al. have provided some very interesting evidence on the relation between trading and nontrading time variances in the French Notionelle futures contract. Although their discussion was focused mainly on the differences between their results and the results of previous studies, however, I would have preferred a more thorough discussion of the differences between their experimental design and the design of previous studies. Because economics is not a laboratory science in which experiments can be repeated under nearly identical conditions, it is important to consider, and in fact take advantage of, the differences in experimental settings when replicating tests of economic theories.

REFERENCES

Barclay, Michael J., Robert H. Litzenberger, and Jerold B. Warner. 1990. "Private Information, Trading Volume, and Stock Return Variances." *Review of Financial Studies*.

French, Kenneth, and Richard Roll. 1986. "Stock Return Variance: The Arrival of Information and the Reaction of Traders," *Journal of Financial Economics* 17, 5–26.

Do Management Forecasts of Earnings Affect Stock Prices in Japan?

Masako N. Darrough* and Trevor S. Harris*

1. INTRODUCTION

Japan's capital markets have played a crucial role in the recent increase in the globalization of international capital markets. As a result, it has become important to understand the similarities and differences in the way Japanese markets operate in comparison to the more familiar Anglo-American environment.

One of the major differences that has attracted a great deal of attention is the relatively high average price/earnings (P/E) ratio for the stocks listed on the Tokyo Stock Exchange (Viner, 1988). A question sometimes raised in the popular press is whether the difference in P/Es suggests that U.S. stocks are undervalued or Japanese stocks are overvalued.[1] Of course, such a question cannot be answered without first understanding the differences in the institutional characteristics of the two markets. Some of the differences raise subtle but important questions, such as whether a particular institutional arrangement can be adopted in other environments. Just as we have seen the transfer of U.S. accounting practices to non-U.S. companies active in international capital markets, certain institutional characteristics of Japan's capital markets might lead to related changes in other countries. This paper considers one such characteristic—management forecasts—which we believe to be a likely candidate for such a global transfer.

*The authors are both associate professors at Columbia University, Graduate School of Business.

We are grateful to Jim Haggard for significant programming assistance, Vic Bernard and Joshua Livnat for helpful comments, the Center on Japanese Economy and Business at Columbia University for its financial assistance in obtaining the data, and the participants at the seminar at Purdue University. We also acknowledge the cooperation provided by *Nihon Keizai Shimbun,* in particular H. Tanaka and J. Uno, for hours of conversation with invaluable wisdom.

1. For a recent example, see ''Abreast of the Market'' in *The Wall Street Journal* (September 6, 1989), pp. C1–C2.

In Japan, the securities exchanges request that management provide forecasts of sales, earnings, and dividends. Although the forecasts are technically voluntary, almost all Japanese companies provide them. In contrast, relatively few U.S. firms seem to publish forecasts.[2] If the Japanese forecasts are reasonably accurate and used by investors, then even non-Japanese companies might be "encouraged" to prepare management forecasts on a regular basis.

Although the evaluation of the relevance of management forecasts is only one piece of a complex puzzle, we believe it is important in understanding the difference between Japanese and U.S. P/Es. Since 1986 the difference appears to be enormous, but there is no consensus so far as to whether the P/Es are really different once "proper" adjustments are made. For example, Aron (1987, 1989) has consistently argued that "adjusted" P/E ratios are virtually identical in the two countries.[3] Others, such as Schieneman (1988, 1989) and Poterba and French (1991), arrive at the opposite conclusion, despite making similar adjustments. All of these calculations are based on historical earnings. Yet, if prices reflect expected earnings, and management forecasts of earnings are relevant in Japan, then it is necessary to examine how these forecasts affect stock prices. This investigation may then help us in evaluating the Japanese P/E "anomaly" in a more precise manner.[4]

Two questions must be answered in order to assess the relevance of Japanese management forecasts. First, how accurate are the management forecasts? If the forecasts are inaccurate, we should not expect them to be useful to investors. We compare the predictive accuracy of management forecasts with a simple random walk model, since all the research we have found on the association between unexpected earnings and security returns in Japan has used such a model as the benchmark (e.g., Ito, 1988; Kunimura, 1986; Sakakibara et al., 1988).

Clearly, although predictive accuracy presumably is necessary (Penman, 1980), it is not sufficient in order to claim that management forecasts are important for investors. Thus, the second question considered is

2. For example, the survey by Lees (1981) found that only 10.4 percent of the surveyed firms (a total of 397 firms) disclosed forecasts. See also the samples in Waymire (1984) or Baginski (1987).

3. Aron's claim is based mainly on two types of adjustments. First, he uses aggregate data to adjust Japanese earnings to conform more closely to U.S. generally accepted accounting principles. Second, he incorporates different growth and discount rates into a capitalization rate. He has made these calculations periodically since 1979.

4. Both Value-Line Investment Service and IBES provide PEs with expected earnings (from analysts) in the denominator.

whether investors actually use these forecasts in pricing securities. To answer this question we investigate whether management forecasts provide additional "news" at the time of their release, by estimating the price reaction around the date of forecast announcement.

The procedure we follow requires a careful sorting of various information releases by Japanese companies. Two disclosure practices must be noted: (1) Many companies disclose parent and consolidated financial statements at different times; and (2) those that provide forecasts announce both realized and forecast figures simultaneously. Disclosure of both parent and consolidated values suggests that there are two potential earnings "news" dates. Simultaneous announcement of both historical and forecast data necessitates that we first discriminate and control for the reaction to the realized earnings. To provide the maximum control for tests of the reaction to forecast earnings, we consider unexpected earnings measures based on historical and forecast earnings as well as the latest "analyst" forecasts.[5] Consequently, the study also provides some evidence on the relevance of these analyst forecasts.

The evidence we provide in this paper suggests (1) that management forecasts of both parent and consolidated earnings are generally more accurate than the widely used random walk model and (2) that investors appear to use both management forecasts in pricing securities.

Section 2 of the paper discusses some institutional background and presents the basic hypotheses. We describe the sample and test procedures in Section 3. The predictive accuracy tests and results are reported in Section 4, and the price reaction studies are presented in Section 5. We summarize the findings and conclude the paper in Section 6.

2. BACKGROUND INFORMATION AND HYPOTHESES

Japan's Commercial Code requires companies to prepare unconsolidated annual reports within three months of the fiscal year-end (FYE). The Securities and Exchange Law, which covers companies listed on the securities exchanges, has also required listed companies to submit con-

---

5. The term "*analyst*" *forecast* should not be interpreted as being equivalent to that in the United States. As explained in Section 3 of the paper, we use the forecasts provided by *Nihon Keizai Shimbun* (Nikkei) analysts. Their officials explained that the forecasts are not made in a manner similar to a detailed U.S. forecast, and frequently are based on management's own estimates.

Figure 1
Flow of information, Mitsui Mining for 1986

5/24/85	7/20/85		3/08/86	3/31/86	5/23/86	7/23/86
A_{t-1}^p	A_{t-1}^c		AFA_t^p	FYE_t	A_t^p	A_t^c
MFA_t^p	MFA_t^c				MFA_{t+1}^p	MFA_{t+1}^c

A_t^c is the actual consolidated earnings for fiscal year t.

A_t^p is the actual parent-only earnings for fiscal year t.

MFA_t^c is the management forecast of consolidated earnings for year t made at $t-1$.

MFA_t^p is the management forecast of parent-only earnings for year t made at $t-1$.

AFA_t^p is the last analyst forecast of parent-only earnings year t prior to FYE_{t-1}.

FYE_t is the fiscal year end for t.

solidated reports since FYE March 31, 1978.[6] These consolidated reports are generally submitted after the parent-only reports, and are required to be published within four months of the FYE.[7]

These two are the only reports legally required, but the securities exchanges require companies to announce a brief summary of current financial information including sales, earnings, and dividends in a press release (Kessan Tanshin). In addition, they *request* management to provide forecasts, and most companies comply.[8] These announcements are made for both parent and consolidated results, so we frequently have two separate announcements and forecasts. Figure 1 provides a summary of the disclosures and their timing for a typical company.

The parent-only report submitted to the Ministry of Finance (Yuka Shoken Hokokusho) is a document with detailed disclosures; the equiv-

6. Although consolidated reports were required from 1978, the use of equity accounting for unconsolidated affiliates has only been required since 1983. Equity accounting is not used in the parent-only report.

7. As of FYE March 31, 1988, listed companies are required to submit the parent and consolidated reports simultaneously.

8. Kunimura (1986) reports a survey that found more than 90 percent of firms (March 31, 1981, FYEs and listed on the Tokyo Stock Exchange) provided management forecasts of sales and earnings.

alent consolidated report (Renketsu Yuka Shoken Hokokusho) contains considerably less detail. The parent-only report generally has been considered to be the one on which many users rely (Viner, 1988).[9] Thus, a question arises as to whether consolidated earnings have any marginal information over the parent-only earnings. Using small samples with historical data, Ishizuka (1987) (event period of one week) and Ito (1988) (event period of three months) show that both the changes in consolidated and in parent-only earnings explain some of the variation in market-adjusted (abnormal) returns. Thus, consolidated earnings would appear to have marginal information content. A problem with these and most other information content studies using Japanese data is that they ignore the forecasts when measuring unexpected earnings (UE). Although Kunimura (1986) and Ishizuka have performed some preliminary analysis on the relevance of parent-only management forecasts, the question of earnings expectation models and the relevance of forecasts in Japan have largely been ignored and remain unresolved (Ito, p. 8).

As mentioned in the Introduction, interest in the relevance of management forecasts (MFs) of earnings goes beyond the methodological choice of an earnings expectations model. We believe it is an important question because the answer not only will provide insights for the analysis of the high Japanese P/Es, but may also influence the institutional setup of capital markets in other countries, as regulators better understand the information needs of the potential suppliers of capital.

The basic question of interest is whether Japanese management forecasts are relevant to investors. This question is broken down into separate pieces that are formulated into three hypotheses. The first relates to the degree of MF accuracy. If MFs have a higher predictive accuracy than a simple random walk model, then we should expect the forecasts to provide a better measure of UE than the naive model generally used. Thus, the first hypothesis to be tested is:

H_1^N: Management forecasts of earnings are no more accurate than forecasts based on a simple random walk model.

The alternative hypothesis is that the MFs are more accurate. This null hypothesis is evaluated separately for parent and consolidated earnings.

---

9. Interestingly, the widely publicized P/E ratios (e.g., as in *Morgan Stanley Capital International Perspectives*) are usually based on the parent-only earnings.

Of course, predictive accuracy alone is not sufficient to conclude that investors use the information. Hence, we next consider whether MFs provide incremental information in explaining the association between unexpected earnings and (unexpected) security returns at the announcement dates. Unfortunately, Japanese MFs are disclosed simultaneously with the other earnings data. Consequently, it is not possible to control for other events in the manner employed by Waymire (1984) or Jennings (1987). To assess the incremental relevance of MFs, however, we need to control for the "news" in UE.

The available research on Japanese securities markets does not provide us with clear guidance as to which UE model to use. In addition to the random walk (RW) and MF models, we have periodic analyst forecasts (AFs) reported in the Nihon Keizai Shimbun (Nikkei).[10] Security analysis in Japan has not developed in the same way as in the United States or Britain. As a result, these forecasts frequently reflect the most recent MFs as extracted from interviews or other management disclosures. At the very least, these AFs should reflect the MFs provided with the announcement of midyear interim results. Possibly as a reflection of the relative importance of the parent-only statements, AFs are only available in machine-readable form from Nikkei for the parent earnings. We were also informed that analysts rarely provide forecasts of consolidated earnings.

Based on the studies we have seen, it appears that there is little understanding of the relationship between (unexpected) returns and the different measures of UE.[11] Consequently, we choose to analyze the question of MFs' relevance for investors in two steps.

First, we consider the impact of annual earnings announcements on returns using different measures of UE. Specifically, we determine which of the three measures provides the strongest association between (abnormal) returns and UE. Brown, Foster, and Noreen (1985) have shown that "the more timely the expectations model, the stronger the association between average cumulative abnormal returns and earnings forecast errors" (p. 8). Hence, the second null hypothesis to be tested is that there is no difference in the association between the different measures of

10. Nikkei is one of two major sources of analyst forecasts. The other is the rival publisher, the Toyo Keizai Shimbun. We do not have access to these forecasts in machine-readable form, but we do not expect that they would be very different given the nature of security analysis in Japan.

11. For a small sample of firms in the period 1976–1978, Kunimura (1986) shows that AFs are more accurate than the estimates based on interim earnings forecasts.

unexpected earnings and unexpected returns. The hypothesis is formally specified in Section 5.

Second, once the results of tests of the first step are obtained, we examine whether the MFs for the next period's earnings have any impact on the unexpected returns after controlling for the effect of UE. Again, this question is considered for both parent and consolidated forecasts, with the latter tests controlling for the results from tests of parent-only forecasts. Thus, formal specification of the hypothesis is also deferred to Section 5.

3. DATA AND SAMPLE SELECTION

The primary research question is whether MFs of both parent and consolidated earnings contain marginal information for investors. Since consolidated data are relatively recent in Japan, the availability of MFs of consolidated earnings is the major constraint in selecting a sample.

The Center on Japanese Economy and Business at Columbia University has a database of parent and consolidated financial statement data, security prices, and "attribute" data (including dividends and parent forecasts) compiled by Nikkei. The database covers a maximum of 10 years (for prices), ending with August 1987.

We first extracted all companies available on the consolidated data file, which runs from FYE March 31, 1978, through May 31, 1987. As 59 percent of all the companies on the consolidated data file have March 31 FYEs, we focused our collection procedures on this subset of firms. We hand-collected the announcement dates and management (consolidated) forecasts released at the time, for all companies with March 31 FYEs as well as for companies with any other FYE whose announcements are published in the daily *Nihon Keizai Shimbun* in May, June, or July of the relevant years. The Nikkei newspaper publication date is one day after the actual release of the Kessan Tanshin.

The "attribute" files from Nikkei contain monthly parent-only forecasts and "update dates," representing the dates on which Nikkei has discussed the company's potential results. In principle the forecasts represent AFs and the update dates reflect the dates on which the forecasts are first announced. However, we were told that the first update after the FYE represents the date of the announcement of earnings (i.e., the date of the Kessan Tanshin) and that this date's forecast is in fact the MF. Therefore, we selected the first update date at least 30 days after the FYE as the parent-only announcement date, and the forecast on that date as the MF for the parent-only earnings. Given that these are monthly data files and that the update date represents the last update in the month, we checked the dates and forecasts against those reported in the daily *Nihon Keizai Shimbun* to ensure that our information is accurate. We found and corrected numerous differences in announcement dates, as a result of an announcement being earlier than the last update in a month, but found no differences in the forecasts. Thus, even when there is an apparent update in AFs after the announcement of MFs in the same month, the actual values of the forecasts do not change. Given that we are interested in both the parent and consolidated data, we exclude observations for which the parent and consolidated announcement dates are less than 12 trading days apart.[12]

The attribute data files are also used to extract the AFs. We select the last update date and forecast prior to the FYE as the most recent AF prior to the announcement of earnings. Although many of these dates are within the month prior to the FYE, the forecasts may not have been revised since the interim forecast by managers.[13] As previously indicated, even when the AF is more recent, it is possible that the AF is based on some updated information from management, so the reference to AFs should be interpreted cautiously.

The final criterion used is that the price and attribute files contain data to calculate a sufficient number of returns to estimate the coefficients in the standard market model used in the abnormal returns analysis.[14] The market model used is

(1) $$R_{it} = \alpha_i + \beta_i R_{mt} + \epsilon_{it},$$

where:

R_{it} is the return (including dividends and adjustment factors) for firm i for day t,

R_{mt} is the return on the equally weighted index of firms in the first section of the Tokyo Stock Exchange for day t,

12. A 12-day period is chosen because the event study part of this research considers a maximum window of -4 to $+4$ days.

13. The AFs and interim MFs relate only to parent earnings. In our sample period, a majority of companies did *not* provide interim MFs of consolidated earnings.

14. Although several studies using daily returns have used returns based on simple price changes (e.g., Ch. 4 in Sakakibara et al., 1988), the returns in this study include all dividends and appropriate adjustment factors.

Table 1
Summary of sample selection procedure

Observations available on consolidated data base	3,488
Observations for which forecasts are not collected	(1,205)
Observations lost by lagging to obtain forecast errors	(752)
Observations lost from lack of parent forecast or	
consolidated and parent forecasts being too close	(150)
Observations without a sufficient return series	(81)
Final number of observations	1,300

α_i and β_i are firm-specific parameters, and

ϵ_{it} is the residual and is assumed to behave according to the standard assumptions.

The model is estimated over the 180 days immediately preceding the maximum event window (-4 to $+4$ days) considered for the announcement of parent-only earnings. Observations are dropped if there are fewer than 90 days of returns available to estimate the market model parameters. The event window is chosen to ensure that we minimize the impact of confounding signals between parent and consolidated announcements.

The imposition of all the filters leads to a final sample of 1,300 observations. Table 1 shows the impact of the different selection criteria, and Table 2 provides some description of the characteristics of the sample. Panel A of Table 2 indicates that most of the observations are in fiscal years 1985 through 1987, which reflects the increased presentation of consolidated data once the equity method was required. This period is characterized by unusually high increases in Japanese stock prices.[15] Panel A also shows that there is a widespread distribution of observations across

15. The TOPIX (Tokyo Stock Price Index) during this period started at a year-end high of 913.37 on December 28, 1984, and went up to 2,258.56 on June 11, 1987. TOPIX is the index (100 on January 4, 1968) of the total market value of the stocks listed on the first section of the Tokyo Stock Exchange.

Table 2
Description of the sample of firms

Panel A: Industry and Annual Distribution

Industry	87	86	85	84	83	82	81	80	79
Foods	21	23	21	2	2	2	2	2	2
Textile Products	13	26	19	1	1	1	1	1	1
Paper & Pulp	7	10	8	–	–	–	–	–	–
Chemicals	29	40	39	3	2	2	1	–	–
Drugs	5	8	6	1	1	–	–	–	–
Petroleum	3	4	3	–	–	–	1	1	1
Tires	3	5	4	–	–	–	–	–	–
Clay and Glass Products	11	13	12	1	–	–	–	–	–
Iron and Steel	16	19	18	1	–	–	1	1	1
Metal Products	17	27	27	2	1	–	–	–	–
Machinery	20	35	30	5	3	1	1	1	1
Electric Equipment	45	66	56	16	16	13	16	14	10
Shipbuilding	2	5	4	1	1	1	1	1	1
Motor Vehicles & Parts	11	14	12	3	3	2	2	2	2
Transportation Equipment	3	3	3	–	–	–	1	1	1
Precision Instruments	9	15	14	4	3	3	3	3	2
Other Manufacturing	5	6	6	–	–	–	–	–	–
Marine Products	3	3	1	–	–	–	–	–	–
Mining	3	5	5	–	–	–	–	–	–
Construction	9	13	11	1	2	2	1	1	1
Trading and Wholesale	27	30	28	10	11	11	10	3	–
Retail Stores	1	2	1	1	–	–	–	–	–
Credit & Leasing	3	3	2	1	1	1	–	–	–
Real Estate	7	7	4	–	–	–	–	–	–
Railroad & Bus	9	13	12	–	–	–	–	–	–
Trucking	7	8	7	–	–	–	–	–	–
Sea Transportation	2	8	8	–	–	–	–	–	–
Entertainment & Service	1	1	1	–	–	–	–	–	–
Total	292	412	362	53	47	39	41	31	23

Table 2 (continued)

Panel B: Descriptive Statistics for Earnings Variables

	1st Quartile	Median	3rd Quartile	Mean	SD
1. Parent-only					
A_t^p	6.73	13.70	24.81	19.40	30.21
MFA_t^p	7.67	14.42	26.77	22.40	34.25
MFA_{t+1}^p	7.23	13.66	25.44	20.34	32.06
AFA_t^p	6.33	13.19	25.01	19.01	29.21
2. Consolidated					
A_t^c	7.65	15.67	28.94	22.21	35.40
MFA_t^c	9.30	17.62	31.80	26.53	40.70
MFA_{t+1}^c	8.63	15.79	29.80	23.96	37.23

A_t is the earnings per share for year t.

MFA_t is the management forecast of year t earnings made at $t - 1$.

AFA_t is the last analyst forecast of year t earnings per share prior to the fiscal
year end.

SD is the standard deviation.

p (c) denotes parent (consolidated)

industries. The electronics industry, which has the largest number of firms, covers a range of specializations including general and heavy electrical equipment, appliances, electronic controls, and electric auto parts.

The descriptive statistics presented in Panel B of Table 2 indicates, as we would expect, that the consolidated earnings are higher (by about 15 percent) than parent-only earnings. It is also apparent that managers are generally optimistic in their forecasts.

4. THE PREDICTIVE ACCURACY OF JAPANESE MANAGEMENT FORECASTS

The first stage of our analysis of Japanese MFs considers their forecast accuracy. Separately for parent-only and consolidated earnings, we estimate random walk (RWFE) and management (MFE) forecast errors:

$$RWFE_{it}^r = \frac{A_{it}^r - A_{it-1}^r}{|A_{it}^r|}, \tag{2}$$

and

$$MFE_{it}^r = \frac{A_{it}^r - M\ F\ A_{it}^r}{|A_{it}^r|}, \tag{3}$$

where:

A_{it}^r is the accounting earnings for the r type report [$r=$ parent (p) or consolidated (c)] for firm i at year t, and

MFA_{it}^r is the management forecast of year t earnings for the r type report for firm i made at $t-1$.

For each firm-year observation we also calculate the difference between the absolute value of the two forecast errors:

$$d_{it}^r = |RWFE_{it}^r| - |MFE_{it}^r|. \tag{4}$$

We compute both parametric and nonparametric tests from d_{it}^r. To reduce the influence of outliers we truncate d_{it}^r at 1 (i.e., 100 percent).[16] The mean of d_{it}^r is the mean absolute forecast error frequently used as the test of forecast accuracy in other studies (e.g., Brown et al., 1987b). Despite truncation, the parametric tests are sensitive to violations of the normality assumption. Thus, we also compute the nonparametric Wilcoxon Signed Rank Test (Lehman, 1975) and the Fisher Sign Test (Hollander and Wolfe, 1973). The Sign Test ignores the magnitudes and reflects only the direction of predictive ability.

Table 3 reports the results of the tests of predictive accuracy. For parent-only earnings all mean and median differences are positive, and for the pooled as well as several yearly samples these differences are

---

16. The substance of the results is not affected by different truncation rules.

statistically significant. In three of the years the median difference is more than 5 percent, so that on average, we can expect these differences to be economically significant.

The results based on consolidated earnings have a similar pattern, although the mean differences are generally lower than in the parent-only case. The differences for the pooled sample of 5.7 percent for the mean and 1.7 percent for the median are statistically significant. Also, in four years the median difference is more than 5 percent.[17] Interestingly, the only year in which the Fisher test indicates a significant number of negative differences (i.e., less accurate MFs) is in 1986. Given the concentration of March 31 FYEs, this probably reflects the unexpected appreciation of the yen in the last three quarters of 1985 and in early 1986, which we might expect to add noise relative to a RW model if MFs had been anticipating a continued yen depreciation.[18]

The results presented in Table 3 clearly indicate that management forecasts are more accurate measures of expected earnings in most cases. Thus, we can reasonably expect that investors use the MFs and that the correlation with security returns is higher for MFUE than for RWUE (to be defined in the next section).

5. THE RELATION BETWEEN UNEXPECTED EARNINGS, MANAGEMENT FORECASTS, AND SECURITY RETURNS

Before we can assert that management forecasts are indeed relevant, we have to consider whether investors actually utilize them. As the MFs are released simultaneously with historical earnings, we must first understand and control for any reaction to the (unexpected) earnings signals. Traditionally, the information content of an earnings signal has been evaluated by the association between a measure of unexpected earnings and unexpected returns (UR) (e.g., Beaver, 1968). The association tests are more complex in Japan because of the separate disclosures of parent-only and consolidated information, coupled with the availability of dif-

---

17. The forecast errors are unlikely to be cross-sectionally independent in each period. However, each period's mean difference reflects an independent observation. Taking the t-statistic for the annual means is 4.36 for the parent-only and 3.65 for the consolidated differences. Each is statistically significant at all reasonable probability levels, so the potential cross-sectional dependence will not affect our inferences (Bernard, 1987).

18. This period of rapid yen appreciation began in early 1985, but was given significant impetus by the meeting of the "Group of Seven" finance ministers in September 1985.

Table 3
Results for tests of predictive accuracy of annual management forecasts relative to a random walk model (in %)[1]

	Mean Difference	't' Value	1st Quartile	Median Difference	3rd Quartile	Sign of Wilcoxon Test Statistics	Fisher Test Statistic
			PARENT-ONLY				
Pooled	6.4	8.94**	- 2.6	2.6	13.4	+**	7.4**
1987	9.2	6.06**	- 1.7	3.1	15.6	+**	4.1**
1986	1.4	1.03	- 10.8	0.0	8.6	+	- 1.6
1985	10.6	7.70**	0.0	7.0	19.6	+**	7.1**
1984	7.0	2.00*	0.1	4.1	12.7	+**	4.0**
1983	2.1	0.87	- 3.7	1.2	9.1	+	0.4
1982	4.4	1.03	- 2.6	2.1	7.1	+	1.4
1981	0.9	0.28	- 4.5	1.7	11.2	+	1.7
1980	13.1	3.46**	4.5	8.4	18.2	+**	4.9**
1979	8.4	1.84	0.2	4.6	10.8	+	2.7*
Aggregate[2]	6.3	4.36**					

CONSOLIDATED

Pooled	5.5	7.45**	- 2.8	1.6	13.6	+**	3.4**
1987	8.3	4.88**	- 0.1	2.2	16.4	+**	2.7
1986	0.8	0.63	- 7.5	0.0	8.6	+	- 4.3**
1985	9.4	6.17**	- 0.5	5.5	18.7	+**	5.6**
1984	8.3	2.79**	0.1	6.9	18.6	+**	3.7**
1983	0.8	0.24	- 3.4	1.3	6.4	+	0.7
1982	0.0	0.13	- 3.0	0.0	3.9	+	- 0.8
1981	1.5	0.46	- 7.7	0.8	10.6	+	0.5
1980	9.2	2.38*	2.8	7.1	17.1	+**	3.4**
1979	6.5	1.32	- 1.4	6.7	14.0	+	1.9
Aggregate	5.0	3.65**					

$* \ p < 0.05$ $** \ p < 0.01$

[1] The differences in forecast errors are based on the random walk minus management forecast. Thus a positive (negative) sign indicates a more accurate management (random walk) forecast.

[2] The aggregate mean and 't' value are based on the annual observations that are assumed to be independent. This test is done to ensure that cross-sectional dependence within each year does not affect the inferences made.

ferent measures of expected earnings. Thus, we have to consider potential information sources in the following order: (1) unexpected parent-only (historical) earnings, (2) MF of next-period parent-only earnings, (3) unexpected consolidated (historical) earnings, and (4) MF of next-period consolidated earnings.

5.1. Test of an Association between (Unexpected) Returns and Unexpected Parent-only Earnings

We first examine the associations around the time of the announcement of parent-only earnings. We have three measures of unexpected parent-only earnings:

$$ RWUE_{it}^p = \frac{A_{it}^p - A_{it-1}^p}{P_{is-5}^p}; \quad MFUE_{it}^p = \frac{A_{it}^p - MFA_{it}^p}{P_{is-5}^p}; \quad AFUE_{it}^p = \frac{A_{it}^p - AFA_{it}^p}{P_{is-5}^p}, $$

where:

AFA_{it}^p is the last "analysts" forecast of year t parent-only earnings for firm i prior to the FYE, and

P_{is-5}^p is the price times shares outstanding for firm i on the day before the first date of the -4 to $+4$ day event window (i.e., 5 days prior to day s, the announcement date of parent-only earnings).[19]

The null hypothesis tested is:

H_{2p}^N: There is no association between unexpected earnings and (unexpected) security returns, so there is no difference for random walk ($RWUE_{it}^p$), annual management forecast ($MFUE_{it}^p$), or latest analyst forecast ($AFUE_{it}^p$) based measures of unexpected earnings.

The alternative hypothesis is that an association exists and that there is a difference. We expect that the association is highest for $AFUE_{it}^p$ and lowest for $RWUE_{it}^p$.

19. We deflate by the price times shares outstanding at the first day prior to the event window to reduce the potential measurement error in unexpected earnings and to be consistent with the valuation relation implicit in these tests (see Christie, 1987). We also ran the tests using alternative denominators. These are: $|A_{it}|$ (i.e., as in equations (2) and (3)) and the price two days prior to the announcement date for the $(-1, +1)$ event period tests, with little difference in the results.

In all the return-related tests, we have to define an appropriate measure of returns. In similar tests using U.S. data, the preference has been to use abnormal (unexpected) returns (AR_{it}) calculated as:

$$AR_{it} = R_{it} - (\hat{\alpha}_i + \hat{\beta}_i R_{mt}), \tag{5}$$

where $\hat{\alpha}_i$ and $\hat{\beta}_i$ are etimated from a standard market model as in equation (1) (e.g., Waymire, 1984 and Baginski, 1987). AR_{it} is also frequently cumulated over a test period to obtain

$$CAR_{it} = \sum_{t=1}^{T} AR_{it}, \tag{6}$$

where T is the length of the test period. CAR_{it} has also been estimated using standardized abnormal returns (e.g., Ishizuka, 1987; Morse, 1981; Burgstahler, Johnson, and Shevlin, 1989), that is

$$SCAR_{it} = \sum_{t=1}^{T} \frac{AR_{it}}{S_{\epsilon_i}}, \tag{7}$$

where S_{ϵ_i} is the standard deviation of the residuals for the market model in the estimation period (equation (1)).

We performed association tests using AR_{it}, CAR_{it}, and $SCAR_{it}$ where $\hat{\alpha}_i$ and $\hat{\beta}^i$ are estimated as described in Section 3. Unfortunately, the market model does not seem to have much explanatory power in Japan (Maru, Sutoh, and Komine, 1986, Ch. 4; Sakakibara et al., 1988, Ch. 2), particularly in certain periods. Looking at our own estimations for each firm, we often find a high variance from year to year in both $\bar{R}^2$ and the parameter estimates of the model. For example, Mitsui Mining has $\bar{R}^2 = 0.10$ and $\hat{\beta} = 2.75$ for announcement date 5/23/86 and $\bar{R}^2 = -0.01$ and $\hat{\beta} = -0.17$ for announcement date 5/22/87. For the sample as a whole the mean beta is 1.32, the median is 0.60, and more than 10 percent of the sample has a beta of greater than 2.5.[20]

As a result of the poor explanatory power of the market model for our

---

20. Sakakibara et al. (1988) in their test of annual earnings announcements find similar results for their sample. In their full sample the average beta is 1.1, but when they remove observations for which the market model $\bar{R}^2 < 0.05$, the average beta jumps to 1.79.

sample, we also considered the correlations between the unexpected earnings measures and raw returns, cumulative raw returns ($CR_{it} = \Sigma_{t=1}^{T} R_{it}$), market-adjusted returns ($MAR_{it} = R_{it} - R_{mt}$), and cumulative market-adjusted returns ($CMAR_{it} = \Sigma_{t=1}^{T} MAR_{it}$), as well as these measures standardized by the appropriate standard deviations calculated in the estimation period (e.g., $SCMAR_{it} = \Sigma MAR_{it}/S_{MAR_i}$, where S_{MAR_i} is the standard deviation of MAR_{it} for firm i).

To test H_{2p}^{N}, the firms are initially placed into 10 portfolios based on a ranking by UE. Different portfolios are established for each of the UE measures. We then calculate the mean and median cumulative (abnormal) returns within each portfolio for four different event windows: $(-4, +1)$, $(-4, +4)$, $(-1, +1)$ and $(0, +4)$. We consider the four event windows because of the perception that there is information leakage of the announcement and also a potential for slow adjustment to news (Sakakibara et al., 1988). However, the purpose of testing H_{2p}^{N} is to ensure that we have adequately controlled for news in current earnings announced simultaneously with MF_{it+1}^{p}. Consequently, we are not really concerned with the vagaries of the event window *per se*. Having considered all four event windows, we choose to report only the results for the $(-1, +1)$ window as this minimizes the omitted variable problem and provides qualitatively equivalent results to those for other event windows.[21] The results of the parent-only test are reported in Table 4 on p. 138. We report only the results using the standardized set of return measures ($SCAR_{it}^{p}$ and $SCMAR_{it}^{p}$), as the other measures yield qualitatively similar results.

The results provide evidence in favor of the alternative hypothesis that there is an association between UE and UR at the time of parent-only earnings announcements, and that the best measure of expected earnings is AF_{it}^{p}. The rank correlation between $AFUE_{it}^{p}$ and $SCAR_{it}^{p}$ ($SCMAR_{it}^{p}$) is 0.059 (0.060), which is statistically significant and is higher than the equivalent correlations for the other UE measures. The pattern of abnormal returns across portfolios follows a pattern that can be viewed as broadly consistent with UE, but does not appear to be monotonic. For example, although the average of the abnormal returns is clearly higher for the top five portfolios compared to the bottom five, portfolio 5 has a

---

21. Of course, information leakage or a postannouncement drift may exist if one looks outside the -4 to $+4$ day period, but this is beyond the scope of this paper; we are considering the market reaction to current earnings solely as a control for other information around the announcement of MF.

higher mean abnormal return than portfolios 2, 3, and 4. Similarly, portfolio 8 has a large positive return despite negative unexpected earnings. This last result partially reflects positive outliers as the $SCAR_t^p$ ($SCMAR_t^p$) for $AFUE_t^p$ portfolio 8 is 0.002 (0.198).[22] Nevertheless, the results reported in Table 4 suggest that we have an omitted variable or that there is a problem with short window association tests.

Given the concerns about market model estimation expressed previously, one possibility is a misspecified model, so we recommend caution in interpreting the $SCAR_{it}^p$ results. But other cumulative return measures provide similar patterns. Another possibility is that net income contains transitory components that are discounted by investors.[23] As previously indicated, we may not have a long enough window to capture information leakage or a postannouncement drift. Nevertheless, the purpose of the test is to control for news in UE. Thus, having found that $AFUE_{it}^p$ is the best measure of unexpected earnings, we can now consider the information content of parent-only MFs and see whether this is a candidate omitted variable.

5.2. Tests of the Information Content of Management Forecasts of Parent-only Earnings

The third null hypotheses (for parent MFs) is:

H_{3p}^N: There is no information in management forecasts of next-period parent-only earnings.

The alternative hypothesis is that there is information in the MFs such that forecasted increases (decreases) in earnings lead to higher (lower) URs.

As already stated, the MF of next-period earnings are provided in the Kessan Tanshin, simultaneously with the announcement of historical earnings. Consequently, to test for the information content in MFs we must control for "news" in the current earnings announcement.

---

22. When we refer to portfolios we drop the i subscript from all earnings and return descriptions.

23. Although some Japanese researchers have used ordinary income as their measure of income for association tests, in Japan the difference between ordinary income and net income includes several items that would not be classified as extraordinary in many other countries including the United States. Consequently, we choose to focus on net income.

Table 4

Means and rank correlations for portfolios partitioned on the basis of different measures of unexpected parent-only earnings (N = 1,300)

Portfolio #	$AFUE_t^p$			$MFUE_t^p$			$RWUE_t^p$		
	UE_t^p ($\times 100$) (1)	$SCAR_t^p$ $(-1,+1)$ (2)	$SCMAR_t^p$ $(-1,+1)$ (3)	UE_t^p ($\times 100$) (4)	$SCAR_t^p$ $(-1,+1)$ (5)	$SCMAR_t^p$ $(-1,+1)$ (6)	UE_t^p ($\times 100$) (7)	$SCAR_t^p$ $(-1,+1)$ (8)	$SCMAR_t^p$ $(-1,+1)$ (9)
1	1.90	0.451*	0.284	2.76	0.264	0.135	6.43	0.147	0.077
2	0.39	0.245	0.066	0.65	0.133	0.054	1.31	0.377*	0.227
3	0.21	0.387**	0.143	0.34	0.422**	0.128	0.70	0.327*	0.073
4	0.11	0.206	0.004	0.13	0.364*	0.125	0.40	0.195	- 0.022
5	0.05	0.424**	0.148	0.03	0.159	0.038	0.19	0.265	0.050
6	0.01	0.348*	0.211	- 0.07	0.109	- 0.313	0.06	0.085	- 0.059

7	-0.01	0.081	-0.239	-0.29	0.224	-0.012	-0.14	0.192	0.047
8	-0.13	0.498**	0.259	-0.62	0.294	-0.010	-0.56	0.264	-0.010
9	-0.29	-0.090	-0.229	-1.18	0.100	-0.062	-1.32	0.319*	0.087
10	-1.74	0.100	0.043	-5.15	0.581**	0.340*	-6.03	0.478**	0.219
Rank Order Correlation[a]	0.059*	0.060*		0.005	0.036		-0.014	0.021	

$AFUE_t^p$ is the difference between actual and latest "analyst" forecast of parent-only earnings year t divided by price times shares outstanding at time $s-5$, where s is the day of announcement.

$MFUE_t^p$ is the difference between actual and management forecast of parent-only earnings for year t divided by price times shares outstanding at time $s-5$.

$RWUE_t^p$ is the difference between actual (for year t) and last year's actual parent-only earnings divided by price times shares outstanding at time $s-5$.

$SCAR_t^p$ is the standardized cumulative abnormal return for year t.

$SCMAR_t^p$ is the standardized cumulative market adjusted return for year t.

* $p < 0.05$, ** $p < 0.01$ for mean not equal to 0.

[a] The rank order correlations are based on the full sample of 1,300 observations.

To test the third hypothesis, we first partition the observations into 10 portfolios based on the magnitude of $AFUE_{it}^p$ as reported in Table 4. Then, within each $AFUE_t^p$ portfolio we repartition the firms based on whether the MF predicts an increase or a decrease in parent-only earnings for the next year. We compute the change in earnings using MF as:

$$\Delta MFA_{it+1}^p = MFA_{it+1}^p - A_{it}^p.$$

Within each $AFUE_t^p$ based portfolio, we expect

$$\{SCAR_t^p \mid \Delta MFA_{it+1}^p \geq 0\} > \{SCAR_t^p \mid \Delta MFA_{it+1}^p < 0\},$$

and equivalently for $SCMAR_t^p$. These results are reported in Table 5. We see that for each $AFUE_t^p$ portfolio except portfolio 5, the abnormal returns for the subgroup of firms with positive ΔMFA_{it+1}^p are higher than for those firms with negative ΔMFA_{it+1}^p. For the sample as a whole, the rank-order correlations of ΔMFA_{it+1}^p and abnormal returns are more than double those for $AFUE_{it}^p$ (0.140 versus 0.059 for $SCAR_{it}^p$ and 0.174 versus 0.060 for $SCMAR_{it}^p$).[24] The results also show that for 8 of the 10 $AFUE_t^p$ portfolios, the negative ΔMFA_{t+1}^p subportfolios have negative $SCAR_t^p$ ($SCMAR_t^p$) and all the positive ΔMFE_{t+1}^p subportfolios have positive $SCAR_t^p$ (8 out of 10 portfolios for $SCMAR_t^p$). Of particular interest is the result for portfolio 8. In Table 4 we report a surprisingly high positive mean $SCAR_t^p$ ($SCMAR_t^p$). When we partition using ΔMFA_{it+1}^p, we see that positive means reflect, at least in part, a reaction to good news in the MF.

The results presented in Table 5 clearly indicate that parent-only MFs have information content. This finding is consistent with the aforementioned belief that parent-only reports are important for users of Japanese financial reports.

An alternative test of H_{3p}^N is to include ΔMFA_{it+1}^p and $AFUE_{it}^p$ as independent variables in a regression model with cumulative (abnormal) returns as the dependent variable. The portfolio results reported in Tables 4 and 5 suggest that the relationship between these variables may not be linear, so standard linear models will yield a poor fit. The results from a regression analysis reflects this poor fit.[25] An observer of the almost exponential rise in Japanese stock prices since 1985 should not be surprised by this result, as earnings did not reflect an equivalent increase.

---

24. The rank-order correlation between $AFUE_{it}^p$ and ΔMFE_{it+1}^p is -0.175.

25. The regression models resulted in insignificant $\bar{R}^2$.

Table 5
Means and rank correlations of adjusted returns for portfolios based on
analyst forecast of unexpected earnings and the management forecast of
changes in next-period earnings, parent-only (N = 1,300)

	$SCAR_t^p$ (-1,+1)			$SCMAR_t^p$ (-1,+1)		
	ΔMFA_{it+1}^p			ΔMFA_{it+1}^p		
Portfolio #	Negative (1)	Positive (2)	Difference (2)–(1)	Negative (3)	Positive (4)	Difference (4)–(3)
1	0.383	0.545	0.162	0.171	0.442	0.271
2	- 0.570	0.806	1.376	- 0.668	0.585	1.271
3	- 0.095	0.641	0.736	- 0.307	0.382	0.689
4	- 0.036	0.298	0.334	- 0.106	0.074	0.180
5	0.482	0.401	- 0.081	0.235	0.118	- 0.117
6	- 0.164	0.470	0.634	- 0.167	0.301	0.468
7	- 0.541	0.348	0.889	- 0.723	- 0.032	0.691
8	- 0.305	0.882	1.187	- 0.395	0.571	0.966
9	- 0.619	0.120	0.739	- 0.732	- 0.030	0.702
10	- 0.288	0.222	0.500	- 0.210	0.122	0.332
Rank Order Correlation[a] (with ΔMFA_{it+1}^p)	0.140**			0.174**		

$SCAR_t^p$ is the (portfolio) standardized cumulative abnormal return in year t.
$SCMAR_t^p$ is the (portfolio) standardized cumulative market adjusted return in year t.
ΔMFA_{it+1}^p is the difference between management forecast of parent-only earnings
for firm i for year $t + 1$ and actual earnings in year t.

** $p < 0.01$

[a]The rank order correlations are based on the full sample of 1,300 observations.

Having established the relevance of parent-only earnings announcements and MFs, we next consider the corresponding questions for consolidated earnings.

5.3. Tests of an Association between (Unexpected) Returns and Unexpected Consolidated Earnings

Similarly to the analysis in Section 5.1, before we can consider the information content of MFs of consolidated earnings, we need to control for any information in the announcement of current earnings. As indicated, we have no analysts' forecasts for consolidated income as these rarely are made. Therefore, the two basic measures of unexpected earnings available are:

$$RWUE_{it}^c = \frac{A_{it}^c - A_{it-1}^c}{P_{is-5}^c}; \quad MFUE_{it}^c = \frac{A_{it}^c - MFA_{it}^c}{P_{is-5}^c},$$

where superscript c denotes consolidated and P_{is-5}^c is the price times shares outstanding on the day before the first date of the -4 to $+4$ day window for the consolidated earnings announcement. Consequently, the second part of H_2^N is:

H_{2c}^N: There is no association between unexpected consolidated earnings and (unexpected) security returns, so there is no difference for random walk ($RWUE_{it}^c$) or annual management forecast ($MFUE_{it}^c$) based measures of unexpected earnings.

The alternative hypothesis is that an association exists and that there is a difference with a higher association expected for $MFUE_{it}^c$.

We use the same return measures as in the parent-only tests. Given the time pattern of disclosures (see Figure 1), it is an open question as to how to partition the firms to test H_{2c}^N. Ito (1988), in a study of annual return associations, partitions observations based on the sign of $A_{it}^p - A_{it-1}^p$ and then on the sign of $A_{it}^c - A_{it-1}^c$. Using a short-event period, Ishizuka (1987), Komura (1988), and Sakakibara et al. (1988) consider the change in consolidated earnings as an independent signal but do not control for other information.[26] Based on our use of a short-event window

---

26. Sakakibara et al. actually use $A_{t-1}^c \times 1.05$ as their measure of expected earnings.

with the sample partitioned so as to ensure that there are no overlapping days between the parent and consolidated windows, in Table 6, Panel A, we present mean values of $SCAR_{it}^c$ and $SCMAR_{it}^c$ (for event window -1 to $+1$) for 10 portfolios partitioned using $MFUE_{it}^c$ and $RWUE_{it}^c$. This provides us with a basis of comparison with the parent-only results presented in Table 4.

The mean abnormal returns suggest that there is no clear pattern in the association between the returns and unexpected consolidated earnings measures. The results using $SCAR_{it}^c$ and $MFUE_{it}^c$ show that three of the five highest $MFUE_t^c$ portfolios have negative abnormal returns, whereas only two of the five lowest $MFUE_t^c$ portfolios have negative abnormal returns. Even if we consider the averages of the top five and the bottom five portfolios, we find that these are indistinguishable. When we use $RWUE_t^c$ as the measure of unexpected earnings, the pattern improves in that three of the five highest (four of the five lowest) $RWUE_t^c$ portfolios have positive (negative) abnormal returns. However, the order of the magnitudes of abnormal returns across the portfolios does not follow the pattern of the size of unexpected earnings. This is reflected in the small negative rank-order correlations of -0.009 for $MFUE_{it}^c$ and -0.011 for $RWUE_{it}^c$. When we consider the associations for $SCMAR_{it}^c$, there is slightly more consistency as reflected in the positive rank-order correlations of 0.038 for $MFUE_{it}^c$ and a marginally significant ($p=0.058$) 0.053 for $RWUE_{it}^c$.

Given the poor associations between traditional measures of unexpected earnings and abnormal returns, and the time pattern of earnings releases, we constructed a third unexpected consolidated earnings variable imputed from the parent-only information. If the ratio between parent and consolidated earnings is reasonably stable, then it should be simple for investors to use the current parent-only earnings to estimate the forthcoming consolidated earnings. Using this logic we compute:

$$PFUE_{it}^c = \frac{A_{it}^c - \left[\left(\frac{A_{it-1}^c}{A_{it-1}^p} \right) A_{it}^p \right]}{P_{is-5}^c}.$$

The mean abnormal returns for 10 portfolios partitioned on the basis of $PFUE_{it}^c$ are reported in columns 8 and 9 of Table 6, Panel A. Although

Table 6

Summary statistics for portfolios partitioned on the basis of different measures of unexpected consolidated earnings

Panel A: Rank Correlations and Portfolio Means for the Full Sample (N=1,300)

Portfolio #	$MFUE_t^c$			$RWUE_t^c$			$PFUE_t^c$		
	UE_t^c (×100) (1)	$SCAR_t^c$ (-1,+1) (2)	$SCMAR_t^c$ (-1,+1) (3)	UE_t^c (×100) (4)	$SCAR_t^c$ (-1,+1) (5)	$SCMAR_t^c$ (-1,+1) (6)	UE_t^c (×100) (7)	$SCAR_t^c$ (-1,+1) (8)	$SCMAR_t^c$ (-1,+1) (9)
1	3.59	0.251	0.229	7.73	-0.099	0.119	5.36	-0.039	0.109
2	0.95	-0.283	-0.125	1.81	0.071	0.066	0.73	0.016	0.048
3	0.44	-0.047	-0.036	0.97	0.132	-0.015	0.32	0.279	0.161
4	0.18	0.097	-0.054	0.53	0.191	0.060	0.13	-0.043	-0.076
5	0.00	-0.392*	-0.181	0.24	-0.152	-0.113	0.02	0.143	0.085
6	-0.17	0.246	0.163	0.05	-0.330*	-0.207	-0.07	-0.138	-0.179
7	-0.50	0.005	-0.119	-0.25	-0.119	-0.115	-0.20	-0.038	-0.154
8	-1.01	-0.001	-0.025	-0.81	0.224	0.092	-0.45	0.130	0.082
9	-1.83	0.071	-0.001	-1.85	-0.111	-0.074	-0.95	-0.291*	-0.251*
10	-6.66	-0.242	-0.157	-6.78	-0.119	-0.121	-6.90	-0.312	-0.131
Rank Order Correlation[a]		0.009	0.038		-0.011	0.053		0.064*	0.076**

144

Table 6—*continued*

Panel B: Summary Statistics
for Portfolios from Sample without Negative Consolidated Earnings
(N=1,190)

Portfolio #	$MFUE_t^c$			$PFUE_t^c$		
	Mean	Median		Mean	Median	
	UE_t^c ($\times 100$) (1)	$SCAR_t^c$ (0,+4) (2)	$SCMAR_t^c$ (0,+4) (3)	UE_t^c ($\times 100$) (4)	$SCAR^c$ (0,+4) (5)	$SCMAR^c$ (0,+4) (6)
1	3.77	0. 133	- 0.086	5.20	0.007	- 0.094
2	1.04	- 0.167	0.002	0.72	0.028	- 0.068
3	0.50	0.018	- 0.094	0.32	0.051	- 0.100
4	0.24	- 0.048	- 0.113	0.14	- 0.390	- 0.139
5	0.06	- 0.326	- 0 .143	0.03	- 0.312	- 0.144
6	- 0.09	- 0.078	- 0.180	- 0.04	- 0.104	- 0.070
7	- 0.31	- 0.200	- 0.197	- 0.16	- 0.018	- 0.248
8	- 0.71	- 0.352	- 0.327	- 0.37	- 0.137	- 0.304
9	- 1.34	0.030	- 0.212	- 0.78	- 0.133	- 0.144
10	- 3.33	- 0.439	- 0.156	- 4.82	- 0.357	- 0.227
Rank Order Correlation[b]		0.040	0.075**		0.035	0.068*

$MFUE_t^c$ is the difference between actual and management forecast of consolidated earnings divided by price at time $s - 5$.

$RWUE_t^c$ is the difference between actual and last year's actual consolidated earnings divided by price at time $s - 5$.

$PFUE_t^c$ is the difference between actual and imputed expected consolidated earnings divided by price at time $s - 5$. Imputed expected earnings is based on current parent earnings multiplied by the ratio of consolidated to parent earnings in the prior period.

$SCAR_t^c$ is the standardized cumulative abnormal return for year t.

$SCMAR_t^c$ is the standardized cumulative market adjusted return for year t.

[a]The rank order correlations are based on the full sample of 1,300 observations.
[b]The rank order correlations are based on the sample of 1,190 observations, i.e., firms without negative consolidated earnings.
* $p < 0.05$ ** $p < 0.01$

the rank correlations are statistically significant at a 5 percent level for both return measures, the pattern of returns is not monotonic across portfolios.

The natural question that arises is why we find such poor associations between unexpected consolidated earnings and abnormal returns. As the disclosure of consolidated earnings is so recent, when looking for comparative results in the literature we could find only three previous studies dealing with reactions to the announcement of consolidated earnings, and all considered the period 1978–1984. Komura (1988) uses monthly returns and cannot reject a null hypothesis of no announcement effect. Ishizuka (1987) considers weekly returns and finds an announcement effect using squared $SCAR_{it}^c$ but does not differentiate according to the sign of unexpected earnings. Sakakibara et al. (1988) find an association using daily CARs and a simple good news/bad news split. However, they find that "the price adjustment to the consolidated earnings occurs on and after the announcement day" (p. 83), which, they suggest, "provides conclusive evidence that the Tokyo Stock Exchange is not all that efficient with respect to consolidated earnings information" (p. 90). Ishizuka's results also suggest that the market reacts slowly to consolidated earnings announcements. Consequently, we next consider whether a postannouncement window of 0 to $+4$ days provides us with a more clearly discernible pattern of associations between UR and UE.[27]

These results are reported in Panel B of Table 6. We report results only for $MFUE_t^c$ and $PFUE_t^c$ portfolios in the interest of parsimony.

The rank-order correlations and the inconsistent pattern of mean values within each portfolio suggest that the results may be sensitive to outliers. Since this was found to be partially true, we only report the median values for the abnormal returns for the 0 to $+4$ event window. We also found that portfolio 10 (i.e., the worst UE) seemed idiosyncratic, so we eliminated firms with negative consolidated earnings from all portfolios considered in Table 6, Panel B.[28]

Looking first at the rank-order correlations, we see that for $MFUE_{it}^c$ ($PFUE_{it}^c$) the correlations are 0.040 (0.035) for $SCAR_{it}^c$ and 0.075 (0.068) for $SCMAR_{it}^c$, with the latter being statistically significant. The median value of $SCMAR_{it}^c$ is negative for all $PFUE_t^c$ (9 out of 10 for $MFUE_t^c$)

---

27. For the -4 to $+1$ event window, the rank-order correlations for $SCMAR_{it}^c$ ($(SCAR_{it}^c)$) are 0.026 (-0.006) with $MFUE_{it}^c$, 0.048 (-0.000) with $RWUE_{it}^c$, and 0.041 (0.025) with $PFUE_t^c$.

28. Neither the median values nor removal of firms with negative earnings provided any clearer

portfolios, but in general the returns are lower for lower UE portfolios. The average $SCMAR_{it}^c$ of the top five portfolios is higher than the average of the bottom five. Similar results exist for the $SCAR_t^c$ portfolios. Thus, there still appears to be some other information affecting the returns.

One possibility is the relevance of MFs of next-period earnings, which is the primary issue in this paper. However, another possibility is that unexpected parent-only earnings and ΔMFA_{t+1}^p are omitted variables; that is, we are capturing a postannouncement effect from the parent-only values. To test this we partitioned the sample into eight portfolios based on a four-way partition on $AFUE_{it}^p$ and then a subpartition on the sign of ΔMFE_{it+1}^p, similar to the process discussed in Section 5.2 and reported in Table 5.[29] We then considered the abnormal returns around the con-solidated earnings announcement date for these portfolios as well as new portfolios based on a further partition using (separately) the magnitudes of $MFUE_{it}^c$, $PFUE_{it}^c$, and $RWUE_{it}^c$ (e.g., the eight $AFUE_t^p/\Delta MFE_{t+1}^p$ port-folios were subpartitioned using $MFUE_{it}^c$ rankings). These results are not reported in the paper because they provide no additional insights. The χ^2 statistic for the frequency distribution based on the signs of $SCAR_{it}^c$ (0, $+4$) ($SCMAR_{it}^c$ (0, $+4$)), and $AFUE_{it}^p$ is 1.30 (2.19), which is not sig-nificant.[30] Other partitions using first ΔMFE_{it+1}^p then the consolidated unexpected earnings measures also added no additional insights.

To summarize, we can (weakly) reject the H_{2c}^N in that both $RWUE_{it}^c$ and $MFUE_{it}^c$ provide measures of unexpected earnings that are associated with unexpected returns, although it is difficult to distinguish between the two traditional UE measures.[31] However, the unexpected returns are not consistent with the magnitudes of either UE measure or the third UE measure imputed from the parent information ($PFUE_{it}^c$). As the objective of the analysis in this subsection is to establish the control variables to use in the test of the information content of MFs, the strength of the association between UE and unexpected returns is important but not itself critical. Consequently, we consider next whether MFs of next-period

pattern of associations for the -1 to $+1$ event window, so we have not reported these values. There was also no material impact on the parent-only results from these adjustments.

29. We used an initial four-way partition to ensure that we did not have too few observations in the final portfolios.

30. We also partitioned the sample into different years and evaluated the UE and UR association by year. There are differences across years, but the qualitative conclusions remain. Thus, we do not report these statistics.

31. The rank-order correlation between $RWUE_{it}^c$ and $MFUE_{it}^c$ is 0.69.

Table 7
Medians and rank correlations of adjusted returns for portfolios based on unexpected earnings and the management forecast of changes in next-period earnings, consolidated (N = 1,190)

Panel A: Management Forecast of Unexpected Earnings

Portfolio #	$SCAR_i^c$ (0,+4) ΔMFA_{it+1}^c			$SCMAR_i^c$ (0,+4) ΔMFA_{it+1}^c		
	Negative (1)	Positive (2)	Difference (2)–(1)	Negative (3)	Positive (4)	Difference (4)–(3)
1	- 0.080	0.288	0.368	- 0.143	- 0.072	0.071
2	- 0.391	0.182	0.573	- 0.058	0.023	0.081
3	- 0.225	0.020	0.245	- 0.019	- 0.103	- 0.084
4	- 0.516	0.008	0.524	- 0.142	- 0.058	0.084
5	- 0.601	0.049	0.650	- 0.322	- 0.116	0.206
6	- 0.310	- 0.002	0.308	- 0.150	- 0.183	- 0.033
7	0.525	- 0.376	- 0.901	0.131	- 0.300	- 0.431
8	- 0.460	- 0.337	0.123	- 0.348	- 0.327	0.021
9	- 0.339	0.180	0.519	- 0.450	- 0.199	0.251
10	- 0.779	- 0.289	0.490	- 0.657	- 0.126	0.531
Rank Order Correlation[a] (with ΔMFA_{it+1}^c)	0.042			0.052		

Table 7—*continued*

Panel B: Imputed Unexpected Earnings

| Portfolio # | $SCAR_t^c$ (0,+4) ΔMFA_{it+1}^c | | | $SCMAR_t^c$ (0,+4) ΔMFA_{it+1}^c | | |
	negative (1)	positive (2)	Difference (2)–(1)	negative (3)	positive (4)	Difference (4)–(3)
1	- 0.361	0.213	0.574	- 0.167	- 0.055	0.112
2	0.106	0.028	- 0.078	- 0.027	- 0.070	- 0.043
3	- 0.015	0.058	0.073	- 0.128	- 0.076	0.052
4	- 0.541	- 0.269	0.271	- 0.232	- 0.120	0.112
5	- 0.297	- 0.312	- 0.015	0.131	- 0.150	- 0.281
6	0.063	- 0.150	- 0.213	0.014	- 0.134	- 0.148
7	- 0.259	0.124	0.383	- 0.349	- 0.180	0.169
8	- 1.147	0.034	1.181	- 0.650	- 0.234	0.366
9	- 0.472	0.155	0.627	- 0.312	- 0.091	0.221
10	- 0.444	- 0.324	0.120	- 0.109	- 0.239	- 0.130

$SCAR_t^c$ is the standardized cumulative abnormal return in year t.

$SCMAR_t^c$ is the standardized cumulative market adjusted return in year t.

ΔMFA_{it+1}^c is the difference between management forecast of consolidated earnings for firm i for year $t+1$ and actual earnings in year t.

[a]The rank order correlations are based on the sample of 1,190 observations, i.e., firms with positive consolidated earnings.

consolidated earnings are relevant, and whether they reduce the inconsistency.

5.4. Tests of the Information Content of Management Forecasts of Consolidated Earnings

The third hypothesis for consolidated earnings can be simply stated as:

H_{3c}^N: There is no information in management forecasts of next-period consolidated earnings.

The alternative hypothesis is that there is information in the MFs such that forecasted increases (decreases) in earnings lead to higher (lower) unexpected returns.

To test this hypothesis we partition each of the 10 portfolios formed using $MFUE_{it}^c$ ($PFUE_{it}^c$) reported in Table 6, Panel B, based on whether the MF predicts an increase or a decrease in consolidated earnings for the next year. We compute the change in consolidated earnings using MF as:

$$\Delta MFA_{it+1}^c = MFA_{it+1}^c - A_{it}^c.$$

Then, within each $MFUE_t^c$ ($PFUE_t^c$) portfolio, we expect

$$\{SCAR_t^c \mid \Delta MFA_{it+1}^c \geq 0\} > \{SCAR_t^c \mid \Delta MFA_{it+1}^c < 0\},$$

and equivalently for $SCMAR_t^c$.

The results for the 0 through +4 day window are reported in Panels A and B of Table 7. For portfolios originally partitioned on the magnitude of $MFUE_{it}^c$ (i.e., in Panel A) we see that for $SCAR_t^c$, in 9 of the 10 portfolios the median unexpected return is higher for the positive ΔMFA_{t+1}^c than for the negative ΔMFA_{t+1}^c portfolios. Similar, though less pronounced, differences exist for $SCMAR_t^c$. Of particular interest in the $SCAR_t^c$ associations is the split for portfolios 2, 4, 5 and 9. In the high $MFUE_t^c$ portfolios (2, 4, and 5), we see that the negative ΔMFA_{t+1}^c subportfolios (column 1 in Table 7, Panel A) actually have negative median values of -0.391, -0.516, and -0.601 respectively, whereas the positive ΔMFA_{t+1}^c subportfolios (column 2 in Table 7, Panel A) have positive median values of 0.182, 0.008, and 0.049 respectively. A similar effect is seen in low $MFUE_t^c$ portfolio 9. However, a note of caution is warranted as there are portfolios, in particular portfolio 7, in which the ΔMFA_{t+1}^c has the opposite effect.

Considering portfolios initially partitioned on the magnitude of $PFUE_t^c$ (Table 7, Panel B), we see that for 7 of the 10 $PFUE_{it}^c$ portfolios the median $SCAR_t^c$ values are higher for positive ΔMFA_{t+1}^c subportfolios. Once again, in portfolios 1, 3, 7, 8, and 9 we find negative (positive) medians of $SCAR_t^c$ for the negative (positive) ΔMFA_t^c subportfolios. The results for the $SCMAR_t^c$ values are similar although the sizes of the differences are smaller.

Taken as a whole, we feel comfortable in rejecting H_{3c}^N, as the results in Table 7 provide reasonable evidence that management forecasts of consolidated earnings are associated with unexpected security returns. However, the conclusion would possibly be stronger if we could more easily unravel the associations between unexpected returns and unexpected current earnings. We believe there are several factors at work that cannot be easily separated. First, and one potentially easy to evaluate, is an extension of the event window. If the consolidated earnings are not quickly priced in the market, then we can expect more noise in short window association tests between UR and UE. However, acceptance of the notion of delayed pricing of information introduces a different set of concerns because it brings into question the relevance of a market price–based association test. It also becomes more difficult to ensure that we have controlled for other information.[32]

Second, and somewhat related, we have most of our observations in the period from 1985 to 1987 (see Table 2). As noted earlier, this is a period of extraordinary growth in security prices (approximately 150 percent) without the same growth in earnings. Clearly, either the market was reacting to information other than earnings or an anomaly (e.g., a speculative bubble) was occurring. Furthermore, in part of this time Japan was faced with a potential crisis in its export industries because of the rapid appreciation of the yen, so we should expect increased earnings uncertainty. Thus, overall, we can reasonably expect the return series to be more noisy in this period than in the 1978–1984 test period of Ishizuka (1987) or Sakakibara et al. (1988).[33] However, this problem should affect

32. Extending the event window by one day to $(0, +5)$ reduced the rank-order correlations in all combinations of UE and UR; for example, the correlation between $SCMAR_{it}^c$ and $MFUE_{it}^c$ went from 0.075 to 0.070.

33. For example, recall from Section 4 that RW outperformed MF for 1986. Removal of 1986 increases χ^2 statistics from frequency distributions based on the signs of the UE and UR measures. However, as indicated, the qualitative conclusions remain the same, so in the interests of parsimony we do not report these tests.

both parent and consolidated earnings unless the latter included a high proportion of export-oriented or foreign subsidiaries.

Third, we use net income as our measure of earnings. As previously explained, an alternative earnings number, ordinary income, excludes items that would reasonably be included as operating income in other countries. On the other hand, net income may include extraordinary items that can add noise to the UE classification. It is also possible that we could improve our associations by using the management forecast from the interim consolidated report. Unfortunately, based on information from Nikkei representatives as well as our own random checks, it seems that most companies do not provide interim forecasts of consolidated income. Given the specific objective of this research, we did not feel it was necessary to try to improve the association between unexpected earnings and unexpected returns by focusing on these two issues.

Fourth, there may be firm or industry characteristics that distort the association patterns, for example, the historical accuracy of managers' forecasts. We shall begin investigating these possibilities in future research.

Finally, given that the problems do not appear to be as serious for parent-only earnings, it is possible that Japanese investors do not yet rely on consolidated earnings for most companies. This is also a question for additional research.

6. SUMMARY AND CONCLUSIONS

In this paper we have identified the information content of management forecasts in the Japanese stock market. Given the typical practice of simultaneous announcement of actual and forecast figures but separate disclosures of parent-only and consolidated figures, a careful investigation is necessary to determine the impact of management forecasts. We believe this is the first thorough study to sort out different pieces of information. The empirical findings demonstrate that (1) management forecasts of both parent and consolidated earnings are generally more accurate than a simple random walk model; (2) the "analyst" forecast of parent-only earnings preceding the announcement date is the most accurate measure of unexpected earnings and is most closely associated with unexpected returns; (3) it is difficult to distinguish between management forecast, imputed (parent earnings–based), and random walk measures of unexpected consolidated earnings relative to their associations with unexpected returns;

and (4) the sign of management forecasts of next-period earnings are associated with unexpected returns for both parent and consolidated earnings.

These findings have potential implications for both academics and market participants. First, for academics, we believe it is too simplistic to use simple random walk models as measures of unexpected earnings in studies of Japanese capital markets. Further, if one is interested in considering price reactions to accounting information, one should control for the concurrent (or, at least, latest) management and analyst forecasts.

Second, for market participants, we believe the results indicate a need to consider management and analyst forecasts in their investment decisions. Further, it would be foolish to ignore the parent-only accounting data, as this appears still to be relevant to Japanese investors.

Third, studies of the PE anomaly should consider the management forecast, particularly if it indicates a large increase or decrease. Finally, for those interested in the globalization of financial markets, it seems reasonable to suggest that as Japanese influence continues to develop, it is possible that we shall see increasing interest in non-Japanese companies presenting some form of management forecast.

REFERENCES

Aron, Paul. 1987. "Japanese Price Earnings Multiples: Refined and Updated." Daiwa Securities America Inc. (May 28).

Aron, Paul. 1989. "Japanese P/E Ratios and Accountancy II: Rhetoric and Reality." Daiwa Securities America Inc. (August 22).

Baginski, Stephen P. 1987. "Intraindustry Information Transfers Associated with Management Forecasts of Earnings." *Journal of Accounting Research* 25, no. 2 (Autumn), 196–216.

Beaver, William. 1968. "The Information Content of Annual Earnings Announcements." *Journal of Accounting Research* (Supplement), 67–92.

Bernard, Victor L. 1987. "Cross-Sectional Dependence and Problems in Inference in Market-Based Accounting Research." *Journal of Accounting Research* 25, no. 1 (Spring), 1–48.

Brown, Lawrence D., Robert L. Hagerman, Paul A. Griffin, and Mark E. Zmijewski. 1987a. "Security Analyst Superiority Relative to Univariate Time-Series Models in Forecasting Quarterly Earnings." *Journal of Accounting and Economics* 9, 61–87.

Brown, Lawrence D., Paul A. Griffin, Robert L. Hagerman, and Mark E. Zmijewski. 1987b. "An Evaluation of Alternative Proxies for the Market's Assessment of Unexpected Earnings." *Journal of Accounting and Economics* 9, 159–193.

Brown, Philip, George Foster, and Eric Noreen. 1985. *Security Analyst Multi-year Earnings Forecasts and the Capital Market.* Studies in Accounting Research #21. American Accounting Association.

Burgstahler, David, Marilyn F. Johnson, and Terry Shevlin. 1989. "Informational Efficiency and the Information Content of Earnings during the Market Crash of October 1987." *Journal of Accounting and Economics* 11, no. 2, 207–224.

Christie, Andrew A. 1987. "On Cross-sectional Analysis in Accounting Research." *Journal of Accounting and Economics* (December), 229–230.

Hollander, M., and D. A. Wolfe. 1973. *Nonparametric Statistical Methods*. New York: John Wiley.

Ishizuka, Hiroshi, ed. 1987. *Jissho Kaikei Joho to Kabuka (Accounting Information and Stock Prices)*. Tokyo: Dobun Sha (in Japanese).

Ito, Kunio. 1988. "The Relative and Incremental Information Content of Consolidated Earnings Data." Mimeo.

Jennings, Robert. 1987. "Unsystematic Security Price Movements, Management Earnings Forecasts, and Revisions in Consensus Analyst Earnings Forecasts." *Journal of Accounting Research* 25, no. 1 (Spring), 90–110.

Komura, Mitsuo. 1988. *Gendai Kigyo Kaikei to Shoken Shijo (Modern Corporate Accounting and Securities Market)*. Tokyo: Dobun Sha (in Japanese).

Kunimura, Michio. 1986. *Gendai Shion Shijo no Bunseki (An Analysis of Modern Capital Market)*. Tokyo: Toyo Keizai Shinpo Sha (in Japanese).

Lees, F. A. 1981. *Public Disclosure of Corporate Earnings Forecasts*. The Conference Board.

Lehman, E. L. 1975. *Nonparametric Statistical Methods Based on Ranks*. Oakland, CA: Holden-Day.

Maru, Junko, Megumi Sutoh, and Midori Komine. 1986. *Gendai Shoken Shijo Bunseki (An Analysis of Modern Securities Market)*. Tokyo: Toyo Keizai Shinpo Sha (in Japanese).

Morse, Dale. 1981. "Price and Trading Volume Reaction Surrounding Earnings Announcements: A Closer Examination." *Journal of Accounting Research* 19, no. 2, 374–383.

Penman, Stephen. 1980. "An Empirical Investigation of Voluntary Disclosure of Corporate Earnings Forecasts." *Journal of Accounting Research* (Spring), 132–160.

Poterba, James, and Ken French. 1991. "Are Japanese Stock Prices Too High?" *Journal of Financial Economics* (forthcoming).

Sakakibara, Shigeki, Hidetoshi Yamaji, Hisakatsu Sakurai, Kengo Shiroshita, and Shimon Fukuda. 1988. *The Japanese Stock Market: Pricing Systems and Accounting Information*. New York: Praeger Publishers.

Schieneman, Gary S. 1988. "Japanese P/E Ratios: Are They Overstated by Conservative Accounting Practices." In *International Accounting and Investment Review*. Prudential-Bache Securities (July 20).

Schieneman, Gary S. 1989. "Japanese P/E Ratios II: Myth and Reality." In *International Accounting and Investment Review*. Prudential-Bache Securities (March 30).

Viner, Aron. 1988. *Inside Japanese Financial Markets*. Homewood, IL: Dow Jones-Irwin.

Waymire, Gregory. 1984. "Additional Evidence on the Information Content of Management Earnings Forecasts." *Journal of Accounting Research* (Autumn), 703–718.

Comments

VICTOR L. BERNARD*

The research conducted by Darrough and Harris can be viewed as having two goals: one long-run and one immediate. The long-run goal is to understand why Japanese P/E ratios are so high, relative to U.S. and worldwide norms. The more immediate goal is to determine the extent to which evidence observed in U.S. markets, including the informativeness of management earnings forecasts, also holds in Japan.

With respect to the long-run goal, the paper concludes that those interested in understanding the relatively high Japanese P/E ratios should consider management (earnings) forecasts. This is a reasonable conclusion, given that management forecasts are shown to be more accurate predictors of future earnings than naive extrapolations of historical data (i.e., random walk forecasts). Whether the use of management forecasts will prove important in understanding Japanese P/E ratios remains an open question, however. As the authors are aware, Japanese P/E ratios have been and are much higher than those in the United States, regardless of whether prices are compared to historical or forecasted earnings. Moreover, the finding by Darrough and Harris (Table 3) that random walk forecasts and management forecasts differ at the median by only 1.6 percent (for parent-only earnings) and 2.6 percent (for consolidated earnings) appears to suggest that the choice between the two forecasts may matter little.

With respect to the immediate goal of extending results found in U.S. markets to the Japanese markets, the Darrough and Harris study has much to offer. There are good reasons to expect that results based on U.S. data might not be replicated in Japan, and there are some important lessons that can be learned from a comparison of the two countries. First, the link between reported earnings and future cash flows is probably much weaker in Japan than in the United States. Therefore, it is far from obvious that the link between earnings and stock returns would be as strong in Japan. Second, management forecasts of earnings are prevalent in Japan, but rare in the United States. Although the evidence indicates that U.S.

*Price Waterhouse Professor of Accounting, School of Business Administration, University of Michigan.

managers provide informative and relatively accurate forecasts (e.g., McNichols, 1989, a concern is that those who willingly furnish forecasts in the U.S. may be an unusual group. Specifically, U.S. managers may choose to provide a forecast only when they are confident their forecast is more accurate than that of the market. Japanese managers apparently do not enjoy the luxury of choosing when they will furnish a forecast. (The forecasts are not legally required, but providing forecasts is a wide-spread practice.) Thus, it is not clear that Japanese managers' forecasts would be as accurate or as informative as those produced by the small group of U.S. managers who voluntarily forecast earnings.

In the remainder of my discussion, I highlight those results in the Darrough–Harris study that present interesting contrasts to the results based on U.S. data, and note one area where my own conclusions differ from those of the authors.

One interesting aspect of the Darrough–Harris evidence is how weak a relation they document between stock returns and unexpected earnings. For parent-only earnings, the rank correlation between unexpected earnings and announcement-period stock returns is never higher than .06 (see Table 4), suggesting that a regression would generate an R-squared less than one-half of 1 percent. In contrast, R-squareds based on U.S. data and announcement period returns tend to range from 4 to 7 percent (see, for example, Brown et al., 1987). One possibility is that the expectation models used by Darrough and Harris are "noisier" than those used in the U.S. studies. However, when I also consider evidence from other studies of the Japanese stock market (e.g., Sakakibara et al., 1988), I would conclude that it is the Japanese earnings number itself that is the issue. That is, the Darrough–Harris evidence appears to reconfirm the notion that Japanese earnings are only weakly related to future cash flows.

With respect to the consolidated earnings numbers, the relation with announcement-period stock returns is again weak. This should not come as a surprise, given that the parent-only earnings are reported prior to the consolidated earnings, and that for many firms the latter may be largely predictable based on the former. To their credit, Darrough and Harris develop an expectations model for consolidated earnings that incorporates information about the parent-only numbers. Only with this expectations model is there any indication of a relation between unexpected earnings and announcement-period stock returns (Table 6, Panel A)—but even that relation is weak.

The key empirical results in the paper pertain to management earnings forecasts. Before one even turns to the stock price reaction to such fore-casts, there are indications that they may offer limited informativeness. Specifically, although the management forecasts offer a statistically sig-nificant improvement in forecasts accuracy over a random walk model in four of nine years, the margin of improvement is "small"—2.6 percent at the median, for the pooled sample of parent-only earnings. One reason for the lack of more notable improvement is that Japanese managers in this sample tended to be overly optimistic (see Table 2). Given that McNichols (1989) finds no evidence of overoptimism in U.S. manager forecasts, this represents an interesting finding.[1]

Even though management forecasts appear to offer only marginal im-provements in accuracy, Darrough and Harris find convincing evidence of a statistically significant stock price reaction to those forecasts, at least in the case of parent-only earnings. The rank correlations reported in Table 5 suggest, however, that the fraction of the dispersion in stock returns explained by the management forecasts is small. Moreover, the results were apparently even weaker before the authors eliminated some "outliers" in the data.

With respect to management forecasts of *consolidated* earnings, the authors recognize that the evidence of a stock price reaction is not strong. Nevertheless, they "feel comfortable in rejecting [the null of no infor-mation content]." I am much less comfortable with that conclusion. In Table 7, the signs of the differences in market-adjusted stock returns for the "good news" and "bad news" forecasts are "incorrect" three of nine times in Panel A and four of nine times in Panel B.[2] The rank correlations between the "unexpected" component of the management forecast and stock returns are insignificant. Finally, as the authors point out, the need to move to a postannouncement period to find any evidence of a relation raises doubts about the strength of the finding.

To summarize, my reading of the evidence is that (1) announcement of earnings affects Japanese stock prices, but the relation between un-expected earnings and stock returns is quite weak; (2) Japanese manage-ment earnings forecasts are more accurate than a naive random walk forecast, but only marginally so; (3) Japanese stock prices respond to management earnings forecasts of parent-only earnings, but the relation

---

1. Earlier studies of U.S. data did find evidence of overoptimism (McDonald, 1973; Penman, 1980).

2. Results based on market model prediction errors are stronger.

between those forecasts and stock returns is weak; and (4) there is no compelling evidence of a stock price response to management earnings forecasts of consolidated earnings, perhaps because these forecasts largely are predictable on the basis of previously available parent-only forecasts.

In closing, I would like to applaud Darrough and Harris for bringing to light new evidence on the informativeness of Japanese management earnings forecasts, and for extending prior research on the relation between earnings and stock returns in Japan. I would also like to thank the authors for helping me learn more about the impact of accounting in countries other than the United States. For several years, I've confronted what has become a common problem in the MBA classroom. I've been facing students who must be equipped to deal with financial accounting issues across the globe, and some students who already know quite a bit about accounting in other countries, and yet I've spent most of my career focusing myopically on what happens in the United States. I'm struggling just to bring myself to a level where I know more about international accounting issues than some of my students, and I know I'll have to do much better than that if I'm to be a successful educator. So I welcome any research that can help me better understand international markets and institutions. The Darrough–Harris paper is successful on that score, and for that they deserve appreciation.

REFERENCES

Brown, Lawrence D., Paul A. Griffin, Robert L. Hagerman, and Mark E. Zmijewski. 1987. "An Evaluation of Alternative Proxies for the Market's Assessment of Unexpected Earnings." *Journal of Accounting and Economics* 9 (July), 159–194.

McDonald, C. 1973. "An Empirical Examination of the Reliability of Published Predictions of Future Earnings." *The Accounting Review* (July), 502–510.

McNichols, Maureen. 1989. "Evidence of Informational Asymmetries from Management Earnings Forecasts of Stock Returns." *The Accounting Review* (January), 1–27.

Penman, Stephen. 1980. "An Empirical Investigation of the Voluntary Disclosure of Corporate Earnings Forecasts." *Journal of Accounting Research* (Spring), 132–160.

Sakakibara, Shigeki, Hidetoshi Yamaji, Hisakatsu Sakurai, Kengo Shiroshita, and Shimon Fukuda. 1988. *The Japanese Stock Market: Pricing Systems and Accounting Information.* New York: Praeger Publishers.

Index

Page numbers given in *italics* refer to reference entries.